CHRISTIAN HERITAGE COLLEGE
2100 Greenfield Dr.
El Cajon, CA 92021

NEW VIEWS OF
THE NATURE OF MAN

THE MONDAY LECTURES

The University of Chicago

Spring 1965

Clifford Geertz
Willard F. Libby
Derek J. de Solla Price
James M. Redfield
Roger W. Sperry
George Wald

NEW VIEWS OF
THE NATURE OF MAN

Edited by John R. Platt 1918-

The University of Chicago Press
Chicago & London

ISBN: 0-226-67080-5 (clothbound); 0-226-67081-3 (paperbound)
Library of Congress Catalog Card Number: 65–24980
THE UNIVERSITY OF CHICAGO PRESS, CHICAGO 60637
The University of Chicago Press, Ltd., London
© *1965 by The University of Chicago*
All rights reserved. Published 1965
Third Impression 1970
Printed in the United States of America

PREFACE

The Monday Lectures were begun at the University of Chicago in spring, 1965, in the hope of initiating a new discussion for our times on the nature of man, his place in the universe, and his biological, intellectual, and social potentialities. The idea was to attempt once more, in the light of new scientific and philosophical and humanistic ideas, to answer the eternal questions, "Where do we come from? Who are we? Where are we going?"

In every major field of the physical and life sciences, in psychology and social theory, in philosophy, in education, and certainly also in technology, the remarkable developments of the last twenty years have led to potentially dramatic revisions in our scientific and philosophical views of what the universe is and what man is, what he can know and what he may become. But too often these developments have been isolated from each other — discussed seriously only within the framework of their individual disciplines and not yet fitted together as they might be into a new and coherent picture of the nature of man. Today we are in the midst of a transitional crisis as we move with halting steps through a time of great danger, unsteadily but surely in the direction of a high-technology world society. In looking forward to the times ahead, in setting up the intellectual and philosophical substructure upon which any coming society must be built, it is evidently of the greatest importance to see if we can arrive at some modern consensus. Our new social structures will be sound only if they are founded on reliable and widely shared assumptions about the moral and intellectual and social nature of man and the basis of his individuality, freedom, educability, and co-operative achievement. Each of the six lectures in this volume is an attempt to bring to the debate a memorable understanding of one particular aspect of the problem and how it is related to the whole. They are attempts to examine successively some of our new views on man's place in the physical and biological universe, the nature of his brain and mind and of his intellectual and scientific achievements, the ways in which he determines and is determined by his culture, and the relation of his own view of himself to his future potentialities.

The introductory lecture, by Willard F. Libby, is on "Man's Place in the Physical Universe." Dr. Libby is the discoverer of radiocarbon dating, the winner of the 1960 Nobel prize in chemistry and of numerous other awards and honorary degrees. He is currently professor of chemistry and director of the Institute of Geophysics at the University of California at Los Angeles. In his lecture he describes some of our new vistas of space and time, man's history on the planet and his newly understood relation to space and the solar system, and how our vast new energy resources and new technological powers are now giving us the possibility of reshaping the planet and ourselves closer to our own desires.

In the following lecture, George Wald discusses, "Determinacy, Individuality, and the Problem of Free Will." Dr. Wald is professor of biology at Harvard and is well known for his contributions to our knowledge of the process of vision and the biochemistry of the retina. He has participated extensively in discussions of the bearing of biology and evolution on the nature of man. In this lecture he describes the peculiar individuality of living organisms: no two organisms are identical morphologically, and no two share the same history. These considerations bear on the age-old problems of free will and determinacy.

In "The Science of Science," Derek J. de Solla Price asks whether we can use scientific methods to analyze the structure of science itself and to analyze the behavior of scientists and their scientific institutions in a way that may be useful in planning and improving our social-intellectual organization in this area. Dr. Price is Avalon Professor of the History of Science at Yale University. His publications include *The Equatorie of the Planetis*, *Heavenly Clockwork* (with Needham and Wang), *Science since Babylon*, and *Little Science, Big Science*.

Roger W. Sperry's lecture discusses "Mind, Brain, and Humanist Values." Dr. Sperry is the F. P. Hixon Professor of Psychobiology at the California Institute of Technology and is famous for his studies of neural growth, the functional architecture of the brain, and the mechanisms of perception and learning. In his lecture he asks whether the materialistic view of mental activity held by some behavioral scientists is adequate to explain the hierarchical-integrative and unitary aspects of behavior. The higher, holistic, responses must be consistent with the lower responses, but they can nevertheless select, organize, and control them, as we find both from experiments and from experience.

"The Impact of the Concept of Culture on the Concept of Man" is examined by Clifford Geertz. Dr. Geertz is professor of anthropology at the University of Chicago and has studied the influence of the Western world on societies in Southeast Asia and Morocco. His publications include *The Religion of Java*, *Peddlers and Princes*, *Agricultural Involution*, and *The Social History of a Javanese Town*. Here he describes the increasingly widespread view that there is no such thing as human nature independent of culture, that man is a kind of unfinished animal still integrating the great recent changes in his brain, and that it is his culture that provides the "control mechanisms," the conceptual codes and blueprints, that he needs to live by more than any other creature.

The last lecture, by James M. Redfield, is entitled "The Sense of Crisis." Dr. Redfield was educated at New College, Oxford, and at the University of Chicago, where he is now associate professor in the Committee on Social Thought. He is a historian and classicist and has translated several of the plays of Aristophanes and Euripides in arrangements for the modern stage. In his lecture he shows how the Greeks moved from their early ideals of order and justice to the later idea that political structures and moral codes were mere artifices, to be ignored by strong individuals; and he seems to be warning that our ideas of progress and of shaping our own collective culture may founder on similar radical-rationalist and anarchic philosophies today.

We are indebted to Sol Tax, professor of anthropology and dean of the University Extension Division, for the generous support of his office in helping to organize the Monday Lectures and to Mordecai Abromowitz, Ben Rothblatt, and especially Talmage Gornto for their handling of the arrangements and numerous technical details needed to make the lectures a success. The lectures are published separately in abbreviated form in the *Bulletin of the Atomic Scientists* in the monthly issues from October, 1965, to March, 1966.

JOHN R. PLATT

For the Committee on the Monday Lectures:
John R. Platt, John A. Simpson, Milton B. Singer, and Gilbert F. White

CONTENTS

1

MAN'S PLACE
IN THE PHYSICAL UNIVERSE

by Willard F. Libby

Man's Environment and Present Situation

I approach the subject of "Man's Place in the Physical Universe" with great hesitancy both because the subject is far beyond my powers and knowledge and because only recently I had occasion to speak on the theme that scientists should stick to their own fields. However, I shall try in this lecture to describe man's immediate environment, in particular as it relates to his function in the present order of things, then to state and describe his role in nature as I see it, and finally to describe his place in the physical universe.

The description of man's environment and present situation breaks naturally into three main parts, as I analyze it. First, it is important to realize that our solar system definitely has time moving unidirectionally from a beginning toward an end; second, life apparently is natural in the sense that all the ingredients except the final magic seem to be present naturally, and life is therefore probably very common in other planetary systems; and third, man himself is brand new on earth.

The first point leads us to the matter of *time, history,* and the *idea of progress.* The earth, as we see it, now appears to be some five billion or more years old; that is, we have a firm concept of a beginning of time. We find that all of our natural time clocks —

WILLARD F. LIBBY is professor of chemistry and director of the Institute of Geophysics at the University of California at Los Angeles.

such as the lead made by decaying uranium and thorium, the argon made by decaying radio potassium, the strontium 87 made by decaying radioactive rubidium 87 — give us the answer that the oldest rocks on earth are apparently around three billion years old; and since the main group of meteorites falling in from space runs around five billion years old, it seems to be a reasonable assumption that the earth itself was formed about five billion years ago. We seem to see most of the other evidence also pointing in this direction — that there was a very different initial state some time ago, that our solar system and our star are somehow running down, and that there will come a time when the sun will no longer shine and the planets will have fallen into the sun. So we see an end to our epoch. In other words, all our indications, or most of them, tell us that time is passing in one direction. It is true that the fundamental laws of physics exhibit a strange property in that they are independent of the sign of time and would allow time to run either way. Some scientists could therefore imagine a steady-state type of universe in which the passage of time was a truly local matter and in which, on the average, there was a steady condition which lasted indefinitely. So we must be very careful in discussing such matters to stay close to fact, for it is easy to turn off into fantasy and metaphysics, where the human influence may be determinative and conclusions may become truly subjective. To be more restrictive about the conclusion we have just expressed that time is unidirectional, we must say that what we know would indicate that this is so in our part of the universe but that this does not necessarily apply in all parts of the universe.

The second point to emphasize is that life is a natural chemical consequence of our planetary environment and in all probability occurs widely in other stellar systems. There is something magic in organic matter which allows it to proliferate in an extraordinary variety of ways. We can only admire the structural beauty and the elements of symmetry in biological molecules and look on in amazement at the delicacy and fineness of adjustment of the structures which constitute our very substance. It is

2

of course an old argument whether a Divine Being lends this magic touch. Scientists can only say that at the moment there is not any chemist capable of doing the magical chemistry which the human body and the bodies of all animals and all living forms perform routinely. We are at the beginning of the time of understanding chemical biology, and it may be centuries before we arrive at the point of being able to make even the simplest form of living matter synthetically. Yet there is a principle here which is difficult to state but which might be called the Principle of Life. Inorganic matter can be converted into organic living substance. Carbon dioxide and water from the air, with a few of the salts from the sea and the soil, together with sunlight, make the green plants which in turn nurture the animal kingdom. Brilliant researchers have elucidated many steps in this magical mechanism, but few would argue against the thesis that there is no one alive today, nor is there likely to be one in the next few generations, who can set up the entire elaborate machine. Nevertheless, the evidence that the process is a natural one is steadily accumulating.

One of the crucial experiments that shows this was done at the University of Chicago twenty years ago by Dr. Stanley Miller, who was then a graduate student, with Dr. Harold C. Urey, who was professor in the Enrico Fermi Institute and the Department of Chemistry. They showed that simple inorganic gases, when mixed and subjected to electric discharges, can produce amino acids and that these amino acids, which are the building blocks for proteins, can therefore be understood as being present — even in such simple systems — and ready for the magic wand or magic act, the life-giving touch which makes the beginning of life. We can see that these foodstuffs, these essential materials from which all organisms feed, are present naturally.

Recently in our laboratory at the University of California at Los Angeles, we have been trying to understand the Miller-Urey mechanism or, rather, the way in which their amino acids were produced. We have taken one of the simplest of molecules, pure methane, CH_4, natural gas, and subjected it to solar ionizing

3

radiation. The solar spectrum, you know, is highly filtered by our atmosphere; but outside the atmosphere we find solar radiations coming in that are so powerful and so virulent that they will ionize, or eject an electron from, anything. In fact, this is the way the top layer of our air becomes ionized, creating the ionosphere which reflects radio waves around the earth, and so on. Solar ionizing radiation, we have managed to show, produces lubricating oil out of methane in good yield. In other words, some two or three dozen molecules can be joined together into one giant molecule as the result of the act of ionization of a single methane molecule. This result was presaged by Dr. Sol. Wexler and his colleagues at the Argonne National Laboratory a few years ago when they showed in the mass spectrometer that the ionization of methane at appreciable pressures caused polyatomic ions to appear. We have also studied the effects of ionizing radiation from radioactivity on methane, and as you might suppose, it seems not to matter how the ions are made — whether they are made from one radiation or another, the results are similar. In fact, methane in the solid state at very low temperatures also produces lubricating oil when exposed to radioactivity.

These results bear on a conclusion that Harold Urey reached a long time ago. He made an almost incontrovertible argument that the beginning of the solar system saw the entire environment in a very reducing state. I must explain what this means. Our atmosphere has oxygen in it and for this reason is called "oxidizing"; the atmosphere of Jupiter, on the other hand, has hydrogen in it and for this reason is called "reducing." Now the remarkable polymerization reactions, such as those of methane which we have been discussing, occur more readily, apparently, in atmospheres which are reducing. So in the beginning, when the ionizing radiation from the sun was perhaps even more intense than now, and there were certainly large amounts of radioactivity present, the conditions for massive production of organic compounds were nearly perfect. Therefore, from these experiments in the laboratory, we deduce that in early times the ocean probably became a veritable soup of nutrient organic molecules. Later, as the sun continued to shine, the hydrogen left the earth because the earth is not quite heavy enough to hold the hydrogen molecule indefinitely; it escapes at the high temperatures of the top of the atmosphere. (This is not true of Jupiter, and so Jupiter still has a reducing atmosphere.) The organic compounds which had been made earlier were then trapped and left behind; they belonged to a reducing environment. In fact, it seems not unlikely that the cementing material which may have held the fine primordial or pre-planetary dust together in the beginning — before gravity could make it stick in large agglomerates to form the planetary bodies — may have been some of these organic compounds which Miller and Urey made and which Wexler and others, including our group at UCLA, have been studying recently. It has even been proposed that this makes it likely that the moon has large amounts of organic matter, just as some of the in-falling meteorites are observed to have. All in all, then, there is little difficulty in seeing that the early conditions that probably developed on earth would support life and that these conditions evolved naturally as part of the whole machinery of planetary and atmospheric formation.

At the same time, however, few scientists have had the temerity to attempt to explain the magical transition from the inanimate to the animate in a scientific way. It is strange that non-scientists are inclined to suppose that scientists are complete agnostics. It seems to me very difficult to imagine scientists not having great respect for the beautiful order seen in nature and for the magic which comes into organic matter when it springs alive. I think that now, as we are coming to understand how the whole stage can be nicely set for the waving of the life-giving wand and the occurrence of the miracle (or however you will describe it), many of us wait with bated breath for some further understanding of how it happened.

Incidentally, very, very few experiments are being done or have ever been done in the direction of trying to generate life. I am not suggesting that this would be a good or fruitful line of research, but it is interesting that relatively few attempts have been made. As you know, life has a particular fingerprint on it. The amino acids in general occur in "optically active" forms, either "right-handed" or "left-handed." For one or another reason, all life on earth predominantly involves one of these two kinds. Amino acids of the opposite kind are generally almost completely useless as food. But we can imagine that life with the other kind could be generated in the laboratory; if we did this it would be the best and clearest evidence that we had indeed generated a new form of life. So the experiment in principle is conceivable, even though it is not at all clear that it would lead to anything useful. I wonder if there may not be among my readers some young man or woman who will think this experiment worth attempting and who will try and do it? What an event it would be in man's history if one could show this step!

You see, a scientist is open to suggestions for experiments! And despite the awe and respect we have for the Giver of Life, perhaps we might still test to see whether we ourselves or chance circumstance might not be able to give life, too. Some may say this is sacrilegious and scold us for attempting it. Fortunately for mankind and the world, we have passed beyond the time, in most societies at least, when scientific experiments are forbidden because of religious or sociological considerations. There is much debate whether social consciousness on the part of the scientist should dictate or control or limit his line of experimentation. I believe you will find that most scientists believe it should not, that the truth is always their goal, and that seeking the truth is their business and purpose. I personally would like to see this great experiment tried with all the modern techniques so that the question of contamination could be handled as expertly as possible.

To return to our main subject, the third major fact about man's place in the physical universe is that he is only now becoming fully acquainted with his environment. He has been here such a relatively short time — as far as we can tell, only a few million years at the outside. The Olduvai Canyon men of Dr. L. S. B. Leakey would seem to have been some of our early relatives,and they are only two million years old. It is by no means clear at this moment just how long man has been on earth, but it seems very likely that our total span is minuscule as compared with that of the dinosaur, which lasted for some one hundred twenty-five million years. We have arrived fairly recently. This is pointed up by the fact that, as a result of the population explosion, today's world population represents about 5 per cent of all the men who have ever lived.

How do we know that man is such a recent phenomenon? There are several distinguishing qualities we humans have, such as the fact that we light fires; no other animals have ever lighted fires, as far as we can tell. Consequently, in field archeology, if a charcoal deposit is found in such a location that it could not have been made by a forest fire, it is taken as conclusive evidence of man. A circular dark disk in the soil five or six feet in diameter is such a find. Likewise, Dr. Leakey's work on the Olduvai Canyon man of two million years ago has depended a great deal on the observance of a notched break in the shin bones of good-sized animals. Such a notch was made by striking the bone with the edge of a sharp rock before breaking it over the knee to expose the bone marrow, which was highly edible and nourishing. When Leakey found these broken bones with the telltale notch, he knew that man must have been there and so began his search for human remains.

With markers such as these and with modern radioactive dating methods, we can trace man's history. The most remarkable aspect is his newness, the awakening and coming awareness we see in our very own day. Within our lifetimes, man has learned to talk through a vacuum over distances of millions of miles by radio and to burn rocks to make heat and power by atomic energy; and he has learned to equip himself better for the use of his unique intelligence in advancing his knowledge of nature by computers, high-energy particle accelerators, and electron microscopes, as well as by television and air and automobile

travel. These developments of our own day add to the tele-
phone, telegraph, and railroad and steamship travel of earlier
days, which are themselves no more than one century old. Earlier inventions, particularly those of the wheel, the building
techniques of the Egyptians, Greeks, and Romans, and the met-
allurgical discoveries marking the Bronze and Iron ages, were
all milestones in man's development. But they were all made
only a few thousand years ago and, most probably, less than
ten thousand years ago in all cases.

In my own research, I have studied some early articles of human clothing — woven-grass rope-sandal shoes found in a vol-
canic pumice-covered cave (Fort Rock Cave) in eastern Oregon
— which are older than all of these inventions but are still very
recent. There were three hundred pairs of shoes neatly stacked
in this cave. By the chance eruption of the neighboring volcano,
Mount Newberry, they had been covered with the best of pre-
servatives, fire-volcanic pumice, similar to that which covered
Pompeii. These were the shoes worn by the first men in North
America, and their dates can be determined very exactly by radiocarbon dating. As a result of such studies, it has been found
that, although many animals were here earlier, man seems to
have come to our continent only ten to eleven thousand years
ago. He came at the end of the last ice age, apparently by walking from Asia across the dry Bering Strait and down the west
coast on a trail which is now fifteen feet under water because of
the melting of the great glaciers of that day.

This man of about ten thousand years ago had great intelligence and capabilities and was physically similar to modern
man. His skeletons are essentially indistinguishable from ours or
the modern Indian's. His shoes were well made, and judging by
his works he was at least as capable in many ways as we are today. This is supported by evidence from the other side of the
world in the great colored paintings in the Lascaux Cave in central France, which are fifteen thousand years old by the radiocarbon dating of charcoal found in dirt on the floor; the intelligence and abilities of the men who made such paintings can

scarcely be doubted. Ancient man — the man of hundreds of thousands of years ago — may have existed in the Americas, but evidence of this is meager; all that we can say is that man appeared essentially in his modern form around fifteen thousand years ago in southern Europe or Asia Minor and spread out from there. In any case, he is young among all the major animals and is changing most rapidly.

It seems likely that we human beings have unique mental and spiritual qualifications and that the theology and philosophy upon which we have been raised are correct in indicating the uniqueness of man on earth. Nevertheless, there may be other organisms somewhere along the evolutionary trail which are superior to man; perhaps these may be found in other solar systems. If in two million years we have come to the point of traveling to our moon, who knows where these superior beings may be by now, if they started a few million years or hundreds of millions of years earlier? One of the truly dramatic experiments we are doing today is listening on radio waves for conversation and intelligent remarks from the outside. It is a very interesting and striking characteristic of man that he recognizes his own uniqueness. But until we understand more about the theoretical limits that intelligent human beings can develop or until we know enough to understand the functioning of our brains, it will be difficult to set any limit on the capabilities of living matter in the direction of intelligence, either the capabilities that lie ahead of us or the capabilities elsewhere in the universe. This is a tremendous new line of thought, and it could guide mankind in the genetic evolution of the future — for as Dr. George Beadle, the president of the University of Chicago, has said so eloquently, man is rapidly approaching the time when he can control his own genetics.

To summarize man's environment: First, we are living in a part of the universe where there was a beginning and where there must be an end. We are in between and progressing toward oblivion; yet we can foresee that some billions of years may lie ahead.

Second, life is a natural chemical consequence of the environment; so we can expect it to occur in the vicinity of many, many other stars. This is what we have called the Principle of Life.

Third, man is new on earth and is a unique form of terrestial life embodying what we may call the Principle of Intelligence.

Application of Intelligence to Matter

Man's role in the development of our solar system is the application of intelligence to matter, including himself. His job is to develop himself for this end. But can he go on developing indefinitely at his present rate of advance? Can we expect that the rate of discovery and improvement in the material aspects of life can continue? Can we hope that our children will see developments as miraculous as we have seen?

The answers to these questions have an important bearing on our outlook. Today it is commonly stated that the bulk of scientific information now being accumulated is becoming so great that it will itself soon slow down the rate of discovery and that no one can hope to be expert in any field or in anything broader than a narrow, narrow aspect of a given field. Yet I would like to speak strongly against this point of view. There is no disputing the fact that the number of pages of material being published in all the various fields of science has grown exponentially and that it is coming to be such a burden that there is grave doubt that anyone could ever hope to read even a small portion of it. This fact, however, does not force us to the conclusion that research must grind to a halt or even that it must slow down. The way out of the maze is a simple one. *True understanding of a subject makes its statement, its description, its definition, and its discussion more possible, not less possible.*

As we come to a fuller understanding of the various branches of science and the various aspects of nature of which they treat, we shall be able to dispense with the bulk of substantiating material which led to the discoveries. Newton's laws of motion made it possible to state on one page facts about nature which

10

would otherwise require whole libraries. Maxwell's laws of electricity and magnetism have had a similarly abbreviating effect. So it would seem that, as we continue to make progress in scientific understanding we can expect the great bulk of material which we now stare at in our libraries to become unnecessary. If we are quick to see the line and quick to develop the evidence to substantiate the new principles and truths we discover, then we need not do any more than write the final summaries, textbooks, or review articles which give the outcome in adequate detail. It is hard to imagine that we could go on forever working on human genetics, for example, without coming to some general conclusions. The conclusions would be simplifying and would then allow us to compress the enormous bulk of literature which is necessary now only because of our ignorance. And so it will be in other areas. It must be. Therefore, it seems to me that there is no real roadblock for the continued rapid development of science and man's knowledge of nature and that we can look forward to its even being accelerated. For success breeds success and gives us the hope that the very outpouring of good things which comes from our mastery can accelerate our rate of discovery.

It is true, however, that there is a difficult problem of communication; for as the world grows, we have more and more people working in science, and the problem of handling the current literature in such a way that one scientist knows what another is doing is by no means trivial. The librarians become very important people; and as all scientists now recognize, it is urgently necessary to develop techniques which will allow us to state quickly and in an understandable way what our new discoveries are.

I believe there are real inventions to be made in this area and that, as time goes on, we can expect that more and more people will find out how to talk with one another. In particular, the language barrier must go down, and we must be able to publish in a matter of days instead of months, and these publications must be available to all — in a kind of scientific newspaper. We get a glimpse of how this can be managed if we think of the rapid copying machines and the effect they have had on our handling of information. Further discoveries like this are possible which will greatly ease the manner of communication. At the present time we sit in a small room and listen to a man speak of his work. Would it not be possible for the man to make a video tape recording which can then be viewed all over the world quickly? I think so; it is obviously so. It is simply a matter of cost. Technically, we are already able to do these things, and as we develop the habit of using such aids, the television medium will come to be employed extensively for education. Television could be a great device for the communication of new scientific results and the co-ordination of scientific research and progress, as well as for bringing home the new results to people in nonscientific walks of life who are affected by these developments. Our present educational television is a very important beginning in this respect. But the main conclusion here is that somehow people will be able to do this kind of thing better and better — that there will be many new methods that will enable us to go on at an accelerated rate and develop new knowledge and new understanding and new benefits from the scientific explorations of nature and thus fulfil man's natural role in the world.

We know much, but the best of what we know is the fact that we can learn and can do research and can engineer and can use our technology. Our great gains have now made all-out war completely incompatible with man's main role — the application of intelligence to nature. The acceptance of this role becomes mankind's great common purpose. When we take this point of view, we realize that mileposts lie ahead: longevity, the cure of cancer, and human genetic improvement. In the field of genetics, for example, we have been very successful with corn, chickens, and cows; so it would seem that we could do something with humans. When we understand better the mechanics of genetic selection, we will perhaps be able to move more wisely, but now we can at least see that methods proved on other animals probably would work on us.

On the whole, though, it is in the long sweep of time that man's true role appears. His intelligence becomes a natural force of the first magnitude. Think, for example, of what intelligence may have achieved already, say on the earthlike planet of some distant star like Sirius. Suppose that for some reason an intelligent being got started earlier there and that he has progressed another million years down the road of time ahead of us. He may have passed a number of mileposts that are only now dimly visible as possibilities in our own future on earth:

A. Perhaps he has come to live in complete harmony with his environment, and to recognize that his true happiness lies in his large control over his environment made possible by his intelligence.

B. Perhaps he has solved the problem of weather control and adjusts the weather to suit his needs, subject only to such natural limitations as the total moisture content of the winds and the total solar energy influx.

C. Perhaps he has modified his landscape to maximize its usefulness and beauty and has moved mountains and made new river courses to fit his broad design.

D. Perhaps he has solved the problem of aging and lives, on the average, one thousand years, dying only by accidents of one sort or another and retaining his virility and his faculties fully to the end.

E. Perhaps atomic energy, both fusion and fission, supplies all of his energy, through large electric-power generating stations and a system of light-weight batteries. Such an intelligent being would have no smog problems, for strict controls would have been put in force to prevent both atmospheric pollution with organic matter and the conversion of this matter to harmful products. In such a world, electric cars would be very popular.

F. Perhaps his planet has no deserts, all land being adequately watered either by the controlled rains or by atomic desalting plants on the seacoasts, from which water is pumped inland by atomic power.

G. Perhaps his population is controlled at a comfortable level by matching birth and death rates. The child-bearing period of the women is extended, and birth control is the order of the day, being accomplished with the simplest of mechanical devices.

H. Perhaps the births are handled by petition to the state and permits are granted only to genetically matched parents. Others must use sperm from a sperm bank to assure genetic matching.

I. Perhaps school and learning are the principal occupations of this intelligent being, taking about half the day throughout his entire life.

J. Perhaps the schools are graded according to age and accomplishment, and nearly everyone is both teacher and student, working to spread useful and happy knowledge as far and as rapidly as possible.

K. Perhaps music and the arts abound and every home has the accumulated lore of the ages in works of art. In such a world, artists would be the most popular and revered group, the scientists and engineers coming close behind.

L. Perhaps the place of an individual on the social and economic scale is based on his past contributions to the society, and honors and influence are synonymous.

M. Perhaps the other planets of this particular solar system are fully colonized even where their environments are hostile to life, with living quarters underground in chambers with controlled atmospheres.

N. Perhaps interplanetary travel is swift with high specific-impulse atomic engines.

All this is not such a great extrapolation. Are not these potential achievements already almost within our reach?

Man's Place in the Physical Universe

I think we must conclude that man's place in the physical universe is to be its master or at least to be the master of the part that he inhabits. It is his place, by controlling the natural forces with his intelligence, to put them to work to his purposes and to build a future world in his own image. The possibility of doing this is exciting. It is what can be done and what may be done if man has the strength to control his irrational tendencies, to suppress his weaker diversionary tendencies, and to develop his strongest and best characteristics. Everything we know would indicate that the opportunities for future development are unbounded for a rational society operating without war. Man's intelligence, self-respect, sense of responsibility, and feeling of destiny are the qualities that will carry us forward. But for all these hopes to come true, man must enjoy his role as king of the universe. He must understand that this is his function; he must have enough responsibility to carry it out without leading himself toward death and self-destruction. This, to me, is man's place in the physical universe: to be its king through the power he alone possesses — the Principle of Intelligence.

2

DETERMINACY, INDIVIDUALITY, AND THE PROBLEM OF FREE WILL

by George Wald

Matter appears to us in a hierarchy of states of organization. Our universe is composed of four types of elementary particle: electrons, protons, neutrons, and photons (these last, particles of radiation, not "material" in the colloquial sense, since they have no mass when at rest, their mass deriving wholly from their motion). Protons, electrons, and neutrons combine to form atoms, the atoms molecules, the molecules more or less well organized aggregates, among them the peculiar class of molecular aggregates that constitute living organisms, and these in turn may form societies.

This hierarchy of states of organization reflects also a temporal sequence. We live in a historical universe, in which over billions of years and vast reaches of space this increasing complexity of organization was achieved. In this essay I should like to discuss two great qualitative changes that have occurred in the course of this development: one, the emergence of morphology, the sizes and shapes of things; another, the emergence of individuality, a universal attribute of living organisms. What we call free will is, I think, an overtone of that individuality.

Elementary particles do not have specific locations, still less specific sizes and shapes. Each is the center of a force field, which can be thought of as spherically symmetrical, falling off in all directions without limit. With these small particles, and particularly with the smallest of them that has a rest mass, the

---

GEORGE WALD is professor of biology at Harvard University.

electron, one is in the realm of physical indeterminacy. That is, one is in the realm governed by Heisenberg's Uncertainty Principle, which states that when one attempts to make measurements upon such particles, the error in the measurement of position, $\triangle x$, times the error in the determination of momentum, $\triangle p$, is equal to or greater than the universal constant of action, h ($\triangle x \triangle p \geqq h$). Since momentum is mass times velocity ($p = mv$, and hence $\triangle p = m \triangle v$), one can write this formula a little more informatively: the error in determining position times the error in determining velocity equals or is greater than h divided by the mass of the particle ($\triangle x \triangle v \geqq \frac{h}{m}$). This says that for any particle of small mass, the more accurately one succeeds in measuring its position, the more uncertain one is of its velocity, or vice versa; and as a result both properties can never be specified more closely.

There is a sense in which this situation can be expressed intuitively. To determine the location or motion of a particle, it must be made to interact with another, at the least a photon or an electron; and for particles of this size the smallest such impact that supplies the desired information so greatly disturbs the state of the particle that though one may learn something of where it *was*, one is made all the more ignorant thereby of where it *is*.

The uncertainties expressed in Heisenberg's theorem are formidable. To specify the position of an electron within 0.3 Å unit (Å $= 10^{-8}$ centimeter) — an interesting amount, since atoms have radii of about 1 Å — it would have to be probed for with an impulse that would kick it to a velocity uncertain by at least 0.24×10^{10} cm per second — about one-twelfth the speed of light. With protons, since their mass is 1,836 times that of the electron, one is better off, yet still in serious trouble: to specify the position of a proton within 0.3 Å would require an impulse that would leave its velocity uncertain by at least 1.3×10^6 cm per second — thirteen kilometers or about eight miles per second.

Such figures hold for the free particles. Fortunately, one can do much better with these particles as components of organized structures, which constrain their positions and motions and take up much of the impulses needed to probe for their locations by oscillatory motions within the larger structures. So for example, we know that an electron within an atom remains in the neighborhood of the atomic nucleus, and much of the energy one might use in probing for its position is taken up as atomic excitation, projecting the electron out to farther mean distances from the nucleus, yet still keeping it within bounds. On the other hand, a sufficiently large impulse to locate the electron more closely ionizes the atom, expelling a free electron that is as indeterminate in position and motion as the Heisenberg principle states. Similarly, one can do much better with the positions of protons — the nuclei of hydrogen atoms — in molecules than in the free condition; and of this more later.

In part, I have spoken as though the indeterminacy principle expresses a failure in physical measurement; but it seems to have a much deeper significance. It is as first stated above — not only that the positions and motions of particles cannot be measured more closely, but that they *do not have* more specific locations and motions. If the uncertainty principle stated only the limitation of our capacity to measure, one might hope eventually to do better. It seems instead to represent a fundamental property of the particles themselves, one from which many of their other properties can be inferred. In a discussion which stretched over many years, Einstein and Bohr argued this point, Bohr maintaining and Einstein continuing to doubt that the uncertainty principle expresses ultimate reality. Most physicists agreed with Bohr, and still do.

Since one cannot specify closely the positions and motions of electrons, one cannot define the shapes of atoms, for those shapes are only the spaces swept out by the motions of electrons about the atomic nucleus. In Bohr's original model of the atom the electrons were described as traveling in circular orbits. Later they were given elliptical orbits. But with the realization that their motions are indeterminate, such models were replaced by the Schrödinger wave function, ψ, and the too graphic term "orbit" was replaced by the noncommittal improvisation "orbital." All that one attempts to say of the position of an electron in an atom is the probability that it will be found at various positions relative to the nucleus, a probability expressed by the square of the wave function, ψ^2. These probabilities define the mean density of electron positions and can be rendered as a diffuse "cloud" about the nucleus, the closest one can come to defining the shapes of atoms. Nevertheless, in these terms atoms do have shapes, and not always spherical. So, for example, p-orbitals are dumbbell-shaped; hence an atom with an external electron in a p-orbital has to a degree the shape of a diffuse dumbbell.

Definite positions, sizes, and shapes come in at the level of molecules. Even here, if measurement were restricted to single molecules, the limitations expressed in the indeterminacy principle would still loom surprisingly large. Consider, for example, a sugar molecule, $C_6H_{12}O_6$, the mass of which is approximately 180 times that of a proton. To specify the position of this molecule within 5 Å — a modest demand, about the width of the molecule — an impact would have to be imparted that would leave its velocity indeterminate within at least 4.4 meters per second.[1] So one would not know where even a sugar molecule is, much less how it is put together, if one could not study it in crystals. The crystalline state helps in two ways: it constrains the position of the sugar molecule to its place in the crystal

---

[1] The numerical calculations may interest some readers. The form of the Uncertainty Principle that best suits the question we ask is $\triangle v \geqq h/m \triangle x$. $h = 6.6 \times 10^{-27}$ erg-sec. To specify the position of an electron within 0.3 Å ($\triangle x = 3 \times 10^{-9}$ cm), since its mass, $m = 9.1 \times 10^{-28}$ gm, $\triangle v \geqq \dfrac{6.6 \times 10^{-27}}{(9.1 \times 10^{-28})\,(3 \times 10^{-9})} = 0.24 \times 10^{10}$ cm/sec. To specify with the same accuracy the position of a proton, since its mass is 1,836 times that of the electron, one has only to divide the above $\triangle v$ by 1,836 to yield $\triangle v \geqq 1.3 \times 10^6$ cm/sec. To specify the position of a sugar molecule, $C_6H_{12}O_6$, within 5 Å ($\triangle x = 5 \times 10^{-8}$ cm), since its mass is about 180 times that of a proton, hence about 3×10^{-22} gm, $\triangle v \geqq \dfrac{6.6 \times 10^{-27}}{(3 \times 10^{-22})\,(5 \times 10^{-8})}$, or 440 cm/sec.

lattice; a probing impulse does no more than increase its oscillatory motions within the lattice. In addition, since in a crystal a great number of sugar molecules are aligned at equal distances apart and all in the same orientation, the measurement has immediate statistical force: it reports the mean condition of the entire collection of molecules, as though one had integrated all the states a single molecule might assume over a long period of time.

Such measurements in the crystalline state specify accurately the mean sizes and shapes of molecules in terms of the positions of their component atoms, which though indeterminate in the free condition, have definable positions under the constraints that bind them in molecules and in the crystal lattice. For every type of atom that engages in forming molecules, one can state its bond radius. Adding bond radii yields the interatomic distances in molecules. So, for example, the bond radii of carbon and oxygen being respectively 0.77 and 0.66 Å, a carbon and an oxygen atom joined in a molecule by a single bond are 1.43 Å apart. By similar means one learns also the characteristic angles between successive bonds. Knowing the bond radii and angles, one can state fairly exactly the sizes and shapes of molecules and construct large-scale models of any molecule one pleases.

A familiar example is water, HOH. The bond radii of hydrogen and oxygen being respectively 0.30 and 0.66 Å, the H-O distance is 0.96 Å. It was a great advance in science to appreciate that in water molecules the two hydrogen atoms are not in line with the oxygen, but make with it an angle of 104° 31'. That dimension is of the highest importance in understanding the properties of water; for much of its behavior depends upon this specific geometry. To give one example of biological interest: water, like almost everything else, contracts on cooling, down to a temperature of 4° C. Below that temperature, however, water expands, so that at 0°, where it freezes, it has a lower density than liquid water. Hence ice floats. If ice did not float, all the waters of the Earth would probably have frozen solid ages ago, and remained so thereafter except at the surface.

There is little chance that life could have arisen under such conditions or having arisen could have survived. This odd circumstance, therefore, seems to have been an important factor in permitting the existence of life on the Earth. Water has this property because its geometry facilitates the formation of a special type of linkage — hydrogen bonds — that interconnects all the water molecules in ice, holding them in a rigid, open structure in which they are less closely packed than in liquid water.

Living cells are molecular constructs. Their detailed anatomy, their relationships with other cells, the course of most of the reactions that occur in them, all depend to a remarkable degree on the shapes of their component molecules. Many of the key processes in living cells depend upon the capacities of specific molecules to fit together closely, a capacity wholly dependent upon molecular shape.

The atoms most characteristic of living organisms present certain advantages in this regard. Ninety-nine per cent of the living parts of living organisms are composed of only four of the ninety-two natural elements: carbon, hydrogen, oxygen, and nitrogen. It is for this reason that the molecules made almost wholly of these elements are called organic and the chemistry concerned with them is called organic chemistry. One of the special peculiarities of carbon, nitrogen, and oxygen is that their bond radii, and hence their interatomic distances in molecules, are almost identical, as are also the bond angles. Hence chains composed of these atoms have an almost identical geometry, whether made entirely of carbon or however mixed with nitrogen or oxygen atoms. Two such chains can fit together, whatever sequences of these atoms compose them or whatever new interpolations of these atoms intrude.

Some of the larger molecules of living organisms — the so-called macromolecules — display an especially intricate anatomy. So for example, the nucleic acids, composed of long chains of four different nucleotides, characteristically take the form of spirals or helices. Deoxyribonucleic acid, DNA, which forms the stuff of genes, characteristically forms a right-handed double helix, in which two nucleic acid chains form a spiral ladder, the rungs of which are made of complementary pairs of nucleotides. This is the way genes are constructed. The genes in turn have as one of their main functions the specification of another type of macromolecule, the proteins, made of long chains in which various sequences of twenty different amino acids are linked together. Proteins again take characteristically the form of a spiral or helix, this time single and very tightly wound.

There was a time when all this was first becoming plain, when I asked myself — and I hope you will forgive the wording, which was just shorthand for what I really meant — Who winds the helices? The answer was not long in coming: The helices wind themselves. The most stable and hence most probable condition for a nucleic acid or protein molecule, or an artificial analogue of either, is to collapse into this characteristic geometry.

This brings us to the borders of biological structure, for such giant molecules, as also some much smaller molecules such as the phospholipids, have enormous tendencies to spin higher orders of structure, highly organized aggregates that at times are hardly to be told apart from the structures of living cells.

A notable example is collagen, the principal protein of cartilage, the tough, glassy gristle that all of you are familiar with through your encounters with the less desirable parts of beef and chicken. In cartilage, as can be seen under the electron microscope, collagen is arranged to form very fine fibrils which have a beautiful periodic structure. One can recognize collagen immediately from its photographs in the electron microscope; and this structure makes a significant contribution to the anatomy of higher organisms. In collagen fibrils we are dealing not with single molecules but with great aggregates of molecules, regularly oriented with regard to one another and regularly spaced as in a crystal. The extraordinary thing is that one can dissolve collagen, so completely randomizing this structure, and then by very simple means precipitate it out of solution, when it reaggregates in this specific, quasi-crystalline condition, hardly to be told apart under the electron microscope from what one finds in the connective tissues of living organisms. There are numbers of other such instances, sometimes involving molecules of quite modest size. So, for example, the relatively small phospholipid called lecithin: one has only to stir this up with water for it to aggregate in the form of beautiful membranes, indeed double membranes, that mimic closely under the electron microscope the membranes found in living cells.

The emergence of size and shape, the progress from an indeterminate to increasingly determinate orders of material organization, represents a great development in the history of the universe. Morphology is a continuous, broadening thread that runs through the whole hierarchy of the states of organization of matter. It is not that the universe has a tendency toward order; on the contrary, it has an overwhelming tendency toward disorder, expressed in the Second Law of thermodynamics. It is only that in the flow toward enormous disorder, and indeed at its expense, a little order is saved out, even a little increase in order. There is no violation here of the Second Law. That little order forms hardly a perceptible eddy in the prevailing flow toward disorder and has been paid for many times over.

I should like to consider now a second great development, the emergence of individuality. The very definition of what we mean by *substance* is that all its molecules are identical. Molecules come that way, identical with one another, and in any pure substance that is the only thing we find.

That is not, however, the way with living organisms. There are no two living cells, and I would venture to say there never have been two living cells, that are or were identical. Even the simplest of cells — any kind of bacterial cells, for example, that one might choose — are never identical. If looking at them through an ordinary microscope does not show that to be true,

23

one has only to go at them with an electron microscope to appreciate their differences.

The position of the viruses is instructive in this regard. The particles of any specific virus are identical, like molecules. It is this property that permits viruses to crystallize, a property that depends upon identity of size and shape in all the particles, such as is not exhibited by any type of living cell. Virus particles are not only identical but static in composition. Unlike cells, they have no metabolism. The only individuality a virus might evoke is in its capacity to mutate; and that is highly restricted, since viruses contain very few "genes." For these reasons, in the hierarchy of states of organization, viruses belong more with molecules than with living organisms.

What kind of thing is a living organism to present this extraordinary individuality?

For one thing, living organisms are enormously complex. They are organized associations of great numbers of very different kinds of molecules, some of them by far the biggest and most complex molecules known to chemistry. Consider proteins, for example. For most of the molecules with which chemistry deals, it is enough to state the elements of which they are composed and the proportions of those elements. For proteins, that is meaningless. The elements of protein structures are amino acids, each of them a molecule of ordinary size. But even this is not simplification enough, for quite usual proteins contain all twenty different amino acids in their structure, whereas what molecules do we otherwise know that have as many as twenty elements in their composition? The enormous complexity of the composition of living organisms in itself makes identity very improbable.

That complexity is compounded by the fact that living cells have not a static but a dynamic composition. They are the loci of a constant inflow and outflow of energy and material. I once heard Albert Szent-Györgyi put this in the following way: If one had the kind of vision that allowed one to see molecules and were in a jungle, one would see molecules wandering about

24

everywhere, at random. In this ceaseless wandering, one might recognize a locus in which molecules of various types were particularly concentrated, which held its form approximately while myriads of molecules streamed in and out; and that locus would be a monkey in the jungle. The continuous inflow and outflow of material, and whatever of its structure endured, would not only make that a unique monkey among monkeys but would ensure that it changed from moment to moment throughout its entire existence. Living organisms are individual not only in space but in time. They grow old; they acquire new characters; they bear the scars of experience — and all these things make them recognizably different at every stage in life.

A further reason for the rigorous individuality of living organisms is that the genetic information that determines them — a monkey, an amoeba, a bacterial cell — is laid out in such nucleic acid molecules as already mentioned, in the form of a molecular tape in which the four kinds of nucleotides which are the units of nucleic acid structures are linked in specific sequences in one continuous chain. It is the reading of those sequences that determines the entire eventual structure and composition, and even aspects of the behavior, of living organisms.

The physicist Eugene Wigner has written an interesting essay in which among other things he said that to any physicist it is nothing less than a miracle that molecular arrangements such as living organisms can exist capable of reproducing themselves.[2] What makes this virtually impossible physically is that the requisite information for self-duplication is laid out in molecular dimensions, held in order only by chemical bonds. Wigner pointed out that this complicated genetic message, particularly because it is of such small dimensions, necessarily must be subject to continuous disordering, so that however well it started off, it could not possibly maintain its order in-

---

[2] M. Grene (ed.), *The Logic of Personal Knowledge: Essays Presented to Michael Polanyi* (London: Routledge & Kegan Paul, Ltd., 1961), chap. xix.

definitely as it was used. For the reason that such molecular information must be continuously garbled, it would be a virtual miracle for organisms genuinely to succeed in self-reproduction.

Fortunately for us all, no such miracle occurs. The genetic message is continuously disordered; that is what we know as mutation. For that reason no organism exactly reproduces itself. All of you know that from your own experiences with reproduction. Always there is something different that emerges, if only for this reason.

That is not at all an imperfection in the order of living organisms. On the contrary, it is what has made them what they are. It is precisely that continuous outpouring of genetic variations that is the basis of natural selection and hence of organic evolution.

The design of living organisms is an altogether different kind of process from technological design. I shall have a little more to say of this toward the end of this essay. Technological design proceeds by setting specifications and then attempting to meet them. Knowing what one wants to achieve beforehand, one sets about producing this result as skilfully as one can.

That is not the way living organisms are designed. Organic design is achieved by the process that Darwin described a little over one hundred years ago as natural selection. It is just the reverse of the technological process. It works by a continuous outpouring of inherited variations, owing precisely to what worried Wigner — the continuous disordering of the genetic message. From that outpouring of variations, the struggle for existence constantly weeds out those things that work less well, permitting those things that work better to go on. In biological design, one is dealing with the works not of a great author, but of a great editor. The whole process is one of editing; and as for the miracle that Wigner called into question, if that ever occurred — if it were in fact possible for living organisms to reproduce themselves exactly — though heredity might seem to be working better, natural selection would no longer work at all.

The disorder in the genetic message is essentially random. It is certainly unpredictable. Since it takes place in the world of molecular dimensions, and involves moreover the behavior of single molecules, it is very likely not only unpredictable but indeterminate.

We have here to face a paradox in a sense, for the genetic disorder that involves the individual organism is coupled with a fantastic conservatism in evolution: the random variation that we encounter in ontogeny, the history of the individual, is coupled with an extraordinary stability in phylogeny, the history of the species. This conservatism, just now being demonstrated, goes far beyond anything we had earlier imagined.

A few years ago methods were developed for determining the sequences of the amino acids in proteins. (As I write these words, the first reports are appearing of similar studies of the sequences of nucleotides in nucleic acids.) Since proteins contain up to twenty different amino acids, which can be assembled in a wide variety of numbers, in any proportions, and in any sequences, it is possible to make an almost infinite variety of different proteins. Organisms fully exploit this potentiality, for no two species of living organism, animal or plant, possess the same proteins.

Each of these protein sequences is determined by the sequence of nucleotides in the corresponding gene. Since there are only four different nucleotides to specify twenty different amino acids, it takes three nucleotides in a row — a triplet of nucleotides — to specify each amino acid.

Let us first consider ordinary mutations in individuals. The blood pigment, hemoglobin, is composed of two kinds of protein chain, a and β, the former a sequence of 141 amino acids, the latter of 146 amino acids. In man, close to twenty different hereditary hemoglobin diseases are now known, in each of which a single amino acid has been switched in either the a or β chain sequence. This is the typical effect of ordinary mutation in living organisms — the substitution of one amino acid for another in a protein sequence. The mutation itself is a corre-

27

sponding change in the determining gene; and that takes the form of a switch in one nucleotide of the three that ordinarily specify that amino acid, since changing one nucleotide in the triplet changes the triplet.

Lately workers have begun to compare the amino acid sequences in proteins of the same type in a variety of organisms. This enterprise is beginning to demonstrate an astonishing result. It turns out that the β chain of gorilla hemoglobin differs from that of human hemoglobin by only one amino acid in the sequence of 146. To determine such a sequence of 146 amino acids takes a specific sequence of 3×146, or 438 nucleotides in the corresponding gene; and as between gorilla and man only one nucleotide has been switched in 438. This difference is no greater than distinguishes the approximately twenty human hemoglobin mutations from the normal; but whereas those individual mutations appear as departures from the norm, hence diseases, the one mutation that separates the β chains of gorilla and man represents the norm for both animals, having become established in both species.

Another closely related protein is cytochrome C, one of the enzymes concerned with cellular respiration and found in all aerobic cells. This is a single chain of about 104 amino acids in a precise sequence and hence is determined by a gene containing about 312 nucleotides in sequence. Between man and the rhesus monkey, one amino acid in the chain of 104 has changed; between man and horse 12 have changed, between man and chicken 14, between man and the tuna fish 22, and between man and the yeast cell 43. The great bulk of such species-to-species changes in amino acid sequence, perhaps all of them, involve changes in only one of a triplet of nucleotides. What this is saying therefore is that as between the cytochrome C of the rhesus monkey and man, only one nucleotide has changed in 312; and as between yeast and man, only 43 nucleotides have changed out of 312. (This is somewhat of an oversimplification, since when so many changes have occurred, some of them have occurred more than once, but this hardly changes the argument.) There was a time ages ago — perhaps one billion years, perhaps longer — in which yeast and man shared a common ancestor. Some of those ancestors went one way, eventually to become yeasts; some of the others took another road and eventually became men. Two pathways lead from that remote point at which we and yeast were one; and that double journey has resulted in a total change of 43 nucleotides out of 312. Surveying all that we yet know of such changes in both hemoglobin and cytochrome C, it appears that, plentiful and common as are individual mutations, it takes about ten million years to establish in a species a single change in the amino acid sequence of the protein, or a single change in the nucleotide sequence of the corresponding gene.

None of us had ever dreamed before that such intimate relationships hold together the entire world of living organisms — that with such vast stretches of evolution coming between, we still retain so close a genetic relationship with yeast. That is a surprise, and I for one am proud of it; but proud or not, the relationship cuts very deep indeed, and once it is pointed out, it ceases to be a surprise, for it is telling us a deep and moving truth; to wit, that we are much more like yeast than we are unlike it.

This fantastic conservatism in evolution, therefore, is coupled with the continuous disordering of the individual genetic message. The factor that reconciles this apparent paradox is natural selection.

I once heard Niels Bohr comment on the highly significant fact that though much of modern physics is concerned with the microworld of small particles, characterized by uncertainty and indeterminacy, all experiments in physics and all the apparatus used in such experiments are in the large-scale, determinate world of classical physics.

We have something a little analogous in what I have been saying. The genetic message is in the microworld. It does not operate statistically but individually. One molecule of nucleic acid or no more than a small number can specify all the protein of a given type that the organism needs. This micromessage, highly subject to disorder, unpredictable changes, probably indeterminate changes, breeds a macro-organism that is submitted to an experiment in the macroworld, the experiment of natural selection.

There is little random or indeterminate or unpredictable about natural selection. Natural selection works on large numbers of organisms to yield regular, statistically valid results. Clearly and definitely it permits those things to survive that work better and eliminates those that work less well. In complicated organisms, a great deal of that elimination occurs before they are ever launched. All of us had already been screened for essential fitness by the time we were born. To have reached the stage at which we could be born meant that we had already passed many searching tests that many of our contemporary embryos had failed. It is estimated that of all the human embryos that begin as fertilized eggs 15 per cent fail to be born.

In a way, therefore, nature, by permitting us to be born, vouched for us; yet only conditionally, only pro tem. Much of the disorder in the genetic message that bred us remains. That is the interesting consideration I should like to discuss next.

There is an exceedingly simple principle that biologists know as the Hardy-Weinberg Law. It states that in any randomly mating population, barring any special selective trends, the proportions in which the normal and mutant genes are represented remains constant from generation to generation. Even if temporarily disturbed, the proportion returns to that constant level a few generations after the disturbance has ceased. Suppose the frequency of some recessive mutation in the population is q, and the frequency of the normal dominant gene is p; then $p + q = 1$. Since the chromosomes are double, each type of gene is represented twice in each individual. Therefore q^2 represents the proportion of persons in the population who, possessing two of the recessive genes, display the recessive character. Similarly p^2 represents the proportion of persons who, possessing two dominant genes, display the normal dominant character. There is also a class of persons who, having one of each type of gene, also display the dominant normal character; these are the so-called carriers, and their proportion is $2pq$. The makeup of the entire population hence is represented by the simple formula $p^2 + 2pq + q^2$ — the fully normal, the carriers, and those displaying the recessive trait. One need only know the frequency of appearance of some recessive genetic trait in the population to figure from this formula the distribution of all three groups.

Consider, for example, the disease phenylketonuria, in which phenylpyruvic acid appears in the urine. That in itself is not particularly distressing, but unfortunately children who display this property also are feebleminded and have a mousy smell. Nowadays such children are helped with special diets. This disagreeable disease is due to a recessive mutation and afflicts about one child in twenty-five thousand in the United States. Therefore q^2 is 1/25,000, and q, the square root of this number, is 1/158. This fraction represents the frequency of the phenylketonuria gene in the population. The frequency of the normal dominant gene, $p = 157/158$. The fraction of carriers in the population, therefore — persons who although normal possess one gene for phenylketonuria and may transmit it to their offspring — is $2pq$ or about one in eighty persons.

Let us consider a second such recessive trait, albinism. Albinos occur in the United States in the proportion of about one in ten thousand; yet that makes the proportion of carriers, computed in the same way, to be about one in fifty-five persons.

At Harvard I teach a class of about four hundred students. They are fine, healthy young men and women, highly selected for their intelligence and other capacities. I go through this computation with them and then point out that on this statistical basis it is very likely that one in eighty, hence five of those students, carry the gene for phenylketonuria; and one in fifty-five, or perhaps eight of the students, carry the gene for recessive albinism. What is more, the five students carrying phenylketonuria may or may not overlap with the eight carrying albinism; the likelihood is that at most one or two carry both.

Obviously such a listing could be extended indefinitely. I

hope that the point is plain. It is that in such a mixed population as ours all these recessives, these products of the inevitable disordering of the genetic message, are quite widely distributed. Very likely none of us escapes carrying some of them. This is of course the trouble with simple-minded schemes of eugenics. The presence of such latent recessive traits, since hidden and almost universal, makes a most difficult problem. However drastically the overt bearers of traits are eliminated, the much larger groups of carriers can be decreased only very gradually.

It is simple enough to calculate the outcome of selecting out of the population some such recessive trait. One such trait, for example, hardly interests us: whether one can or cannot taste the chemical substance phenylthiocarbamide (PTC). Some people taste it as very bitter, others not at all. The ability to taste PTC is a dominant trait, non-tasting a recessive. About 30 per cent of Americans are non-tasters.

Suppose one set about preventing anyone who could not taste PTC from having offspring. It turns out that it would take approximately one thousand generations, not even then to eliminate non-tasters, but to lower the frequency of that non-taster gene in the population from its present value of 55 per cent to about 1/1000. If we count thirty years to a generation, one thousand generations would bring us back to about thirty thousand years ago, when Cro-Magnon man was painting those interesting pictures on the walls of caves in the Dordogne.

(That thought inspires a digression. Many of us nowadays feel as though we were virtually drowning in humanity. The present population of the earth is something over three billion. It is possible to achieve a more satisfying sense of individuality by regarding one's status in time rather than in space — seeing oneself at the head of a procession of ancestors rather than one among the crowd of one's contemporaries. It is rather astonishing to realize that only one hundred ancestors in line carry one back to about 1000 B.C. That isn't very many ancestors. One could have known that many persons fairly intimately, and valued their opinions, and hoped that one would not disappoint them.)

Note also that however far one pursued so rigorous a eugenic enterprise, however purified the stock one finally achieved, the continuous disordering of the genetic message by mutation would keep the problem alive. The testing for and weeding out of new mutants would have to go on forever.

Why make such a point of the undesirable character of mutations? It is because almost all mutations are disadvantageous, and the great bulk of them are also recessive. Natural selection has already singled out the most advantageous traits that a species can evoke, and not only made them the norm but gradually made them dominant. Drastic change in the conditions of life — a great change of climate, the colonization of new territory, the advent of a new predator — by changing the criteria of selection, might make a hitherto harmful mutation advantageous; and after a time, it might be selected into dominance. But barring such changes in environment, mutations are almost always disadvantageous and generally recessive.

To return to our main argument: through the factors we have been discussing, the complexity of the organism, its dynamic state, and the constant intrusion of genetic disorder, one can be quite convinced that each living thing, including every man, is unique, an individual unlike any other in space or time. But to those factors one must add another of ultimate importance. It is that living organisms store history. Not only does each of us come into the world with a unique composition and inheritance, but to those we begin to accumulate a unique experience. That personal history, growing throughout our lives, is ours alone. That private self that is you or I is the unique composition and structure that come to us via metabolism and inheritance, coupled with a unique personal history that is forever growing.

Our storing of history, like our other attributes, has both phylogenetic and ontogenetic aspects. I have already spoken of its status in evolution, the extraordinary conservatism in our genetic makeup that makes us kin with all other living creatures, even with yeast. No one yet knows the physical basis of our capacity to store history as individuals, to learn and remember, and to develop new patterns of behavior on the basis of our experience.

I should be willing to assume as a hypothesis that all those things that go into composing the private self are determinate. One consideration that inclines me toward that view is that all the processes I know of in living organisms are multimolecular. Usually they involve millions if not billions of molecules. Any process of that nature has a regularity that comes out of its statistics, a regularity that would disappear the moment that one went over from processes involving large numbers of molecules to those involving one or a few molecules.

Why do I make so much of this matter of the way large collections of molecules behave as compared with one or a few? Consider a hypothetical chemical reaction $A \rightarrow B$ in which a very large number of molecules are involved, perhaps several million. I should have no trouble measuring its course, which I would find to be very regular. Measuring, for example, the decline in precursor A with time, beginning with all A, I would obtain a regular die-away curve.

Suppose, however, that I begin to divide A among many little separate compartments (for example, test tubes). I keep on dividing until finally only one or a few molecules of A are in each test tube. Taking all the test tubes together, the reaction $A \rightarrow B$ would of course proceed exactly as before. Let us assume that it is a reasonably fast process, finished in one hour. If I have so much subdivided the population of molecules that I have a test tube containing just one molecule of A, and I watch that one molecule, I will see that at some moment — any moment from the beginning of the reaction to an hour later — that one molecule of A will suddenly and instantaneously pop over to B. It might remain A for forty seconds or forty minutes, and then suddenly, for no reason I can say, it is B.

The point I am trying to make is that when we are dealing with many millions of molecules, and hence the statistics of large numbers, one has a show of smoothness, predictability, and complete determinacy. The moment one's attention is fastened on one molecule in a population — one need not isolate that molecule but only concentrate one's attention upon it — all that regularity and dependability disappear. Now it's all-or-nothing: it's either A or B and goes from one to the other in an instant. What is a smooth and predictable process in large numbers of units becomes an all-or-nothing, explosive and unpredictable transition in a single unit.

Hence it would be an important consideration in our problem if one had any reason to suppose that there are processes governing, for example, our behavior that depend upon reactions of one or a few molecules. It so happens that my work on vision has brought me together with what is perhaps the nearest known approach to such a process. Our vision in dim light — our night vision — depends upon receptor cells in the retina known as rods. We have known for some years that each of these rods, when completely dark-adapted, can be stimulated by absorbing one photon, one quantum of light — the smallest quantity of light that can exist. That one quantum of light is absorbed by one molecule of the visual pigment rhodopsin. I do not know of any other process in living organisms that has been demonstrated to get down to that level.

If that absorption of one quantum of light by one molecule in a human rod made us see — brought that response into consciousness — then our seeing, at least at the threshold level in the dark-adapted eye, would be explosive, unpredictable, and indeterminate, as fortunately it is not. The situation is in fact somewhat worse than I have described. Molecules of rhodopsin are intrinsically somewhat unstable, and since there are many billions of them in the retina, one of them is likely to disintegrate at any moment, even in the complete absence of light. Since that may be all that is needed to excite a rod, any given rod may respond at any moment, even in the dark. That makes for a dark "noise level." Fortunately, however, the stimulation of single rods, or their responding without stimulation, is not

enough to make us see, and none of our behavior depends upon
it. For us to see, about ten rods must respond, within a very
small space of retina and within a small fraction of a second.
This is the built-in factor of safety — what radio engineers
would recognize as a signal-to-noise ratio — that ensures that
when we see, it is no accident but a genuine response to light.
Even in this instance, therefore, there is a safeguard; and the
potential indeterminacy is rendered reasonably determinate by
the insistence upon a degree of simultaneity and contiguity in
space that puts the process beyond chance and makes of it a
reliable basis for behavior.

For these and other reasons I assume that all our behavior is
determined. That may in itself seem to some an unpalatable assumption, one that threatens to deprive us of some precious
measure of freedom. I doubt that it does; but in that connection
I should like to note that, however firmly a man may insist upon
his free will at other times, he is a rigid determinist when making an alibi. The entire attitude of excuse — the plea of irre-
sponsibility, extenuating circumstances, unforeseen events —
rests on the thesis that, however much the defendant willed an
act, forces beyond his control prevented it. We boast of free will
whenever we take pride in our actions; but our alibis are all
confessions of determinism.

Actually, I see no essential incompatibility between such a
complete determinism of behavior and free will. Behavior may
all be determined, but it is surely not all predictable; and I think
that the essence of our free will lies in that unpredictability.

We have spent some time above establishing in some detail
our uniqueness as individuals and our essential unpredictability. Each of us possesses a unique composition that changes from
moment to moment. Each of us carries also a unique genetic
complement that, what with recessives that are not expressed
and dominant genes that for some unknown reason withhold
their effects, remains to a large degree hidden. All of us bear
hereditary potentials that we know nothing about and will

never find anything about. Furthermore, we store history, a continuous flow of experience. When the time comes to make a decision, to exercise what we call free will, to choose — when that time comes, the self that exercises free will is, I think, that unique private self, that unique product of the unique composition, genetics and history, all to a degree unknown. At that moment no one can predict the outcome, neither an outsider nor the person making the decision, because no one has the requisite information. So I should say that the essence of free will is not a failure of determinism but a failure of predictability.

How free is free will? It is rather curious that, for all the enthusiasm it arouses, it involves so narrow a segment of our experience and choice. A large realm of our behavior is completely determined and predictable; it is that which permits us to go on living as organized and integrated beings. There is, for example, all the interplay and mutual adjustment of our parts that permits them to function together harmoniously, all the internal adjustment that constitutes our vegetative life. None of that calls for decisions; those functions are too important for decision and are safeguarded by being made automatic.

The Englishman Francis Galton decided one day to perform the experiment of never drawing another breath without willing it. He went along happily doing this for awhile: he willed a breath and then drew it; then he willed the next breath and drew it. Finally, thinking he had had enough of that, he stopped willing and promptly stopped breathing. He described going through a "terrible half hour" in serious danger of suffocating; having intruded upon one of the automatic, vegetative functions, he found it hard to get out of the way again, and let it go on.[3]

A second series of relationships is bound up with the endless need to function in an environment that includes other creatures of the same kind, creatures of other kinds, food-getting,

---

[3] Francis Galton, *Memories of My Life* (London: Methuen, 1908), p. 276.

reproduction — all the things that, apart from one's internal organization, let one hold a place in the world. Some aspects of those relationships involve choice, but many others involve necessity.

So, for example, about half a century ago two great physiologists, Anton Carlson in Chicago and Walter Cannon at Harvard, were conducting their classic experiments on hunger. Both workers took pains to define what they meant by hunger, particularly the distinction between hunger and appetite. I think it was Cannon who put this distinction: "Appetite invites one to eat, but hunger forces one to eat." Under the impetus of hunger, an animal is not asked but ordered to eat; and hungry persons will then eat things that disgust them, that may even make them violently ill.

There is a third realm of behavior that may lie beyond choice, that emerges most clearly when the welfare of the individual is pitted against that of the group — the society, or perhaps the species. Some years ago I was involved in experiments with rats that showed that a variety of essential nutritional deprivations — lack of food, lack of water, or lack of certain essential vitamins — had the invariable effect of forcing them to run. Such deprived rats, given access to a running wheel, ran up to forty times as much as well-fed animals, and as a result petered out ever so much more quickly than if they had remained quiet.[4] On looking through the literature I learned that the universal sign of hunger in animals from protozoa to man is increased activity.

What is its point? I think that the running of a hungry rat in a wheel is a model in small for the well-known ecological phenomenon of hunger migration. The most famous such migration is that of the lemmings, large rodents that live high up on the mountainsides of Norway. Periodically, roughly every decade, the lemming population becomes too dense for its food resources. A hungry lemming is forced into hunger activity; it is

---

[4] G. Wald and B. Jackson, "Activity and Nutritional Deprivation," *Proceedings of the National Academy of Sciences*, XXX (1944), 255.

driven to run, apparently quite aimlessly. Under this compulsion great numbers of lemmings leave their centers of population. Owing to the geography of Norway, many of them, coming down off the mountainsides, reach the ocean, and swimming out perish there. They do not seek the ocean; other lemmings that live on the other side of the same mountains, wander off to perish on the plains of Lapland. The migration continues, impelled by this forced activity, until the population has been so thinned out at its center that there is now enough food for those that remain. Then the migration automatically stops.

The point of such a migration is not, as one might first suppose, to search out new sources of food or new places to live. If there were such places, lemmings would have occupied them long before. The point of this behavior is not to rescue the migrating individuals but to eliminate them, to the advantage of the species. Apparently, no hunger migrations end in successful colonization; they end invariably in destroying the migrating animals.[5]

Large portions of our behavior therefore do not call for decision and are not free. The bulk of our internal regulation is of this nature, as also much of our traffic with the external world and as, finally, a complex of special demands calculated more to serve the welfare of the group or species than that of the individual. (It is hard to avoid remarking parallels between this tripartite division of behavior and Freud's id, ego, and superego.) I would suppose that such forced and automatic activities account for most of our behavior.

At best, therefore, our will is free only within limits. The more one thinks about it, the more one realizes how narrow those limits are. Most of our decisions involve only the choice between two alternatives. The tendency to make such choices and judgments is so marked that sometimes I think the whole

---

[5] W. Heape, *Emigration, Migration, and Nomadism* (Cambridge: Heffer & Sons, 1931), p. 21: "The act of mass emigration . . . is performed by a surplus population. . . . The main incitement . . . would appear to be want of food . . . and the result in the end is inevitably disaster."

nervous system must be made up of nerve fibers that bifurcate, one branch saying "either," the other saying "or." How often must we decide between more than two possibilities? Three possibilities to choose among make an almost unbearably complicated situation.

One realizes by this within what narrow constraints our freedom of will operates. It does not ordinarily range widely at all. Yet, such as it is, it is important and precious to us and, I think, real — real in the sense that I have tried to define, its freedom residing in its unpredictability.

It should be noted that this basis for free will would not deny it to other creatures than man. The behavior of any other living organism is as likely as human behavior to be determined and as likely to thwart prediction. It is this essential unpredictability of animal behavior that led an exasperated physiologist some years ago to state what came to be called the Harvard Law of Animal Behavior: "Under precisely controlled conditions, an animal does as it damn pleases." Could one ask more free will than that?

Let me mention here another aspect of our individuality that merits attention. Scientists make much of the verifiability of their experiments and observations. One person having discovered something, others can duplicate this result. If that were in fact duplication, however, if it involved really repeating the identical experience, there would be no verification in it at all. It would be mere duplication — like another pressing of the same phonograph record or another copy of the same printed page. Information is not increased by simple repetition.

It is precisely the uniqueness of each scientist, the fact that what each one does is necessarily somewhat different from what any other scientist might do, that brings forth the wonderful result, a common area of agreement among several observers, each distinct and unique. It is only the differences among the observers that gives their agreement the force of verification.

I should like to mention a further consideration. There is a kind of indeterminacy that involves human behavior — and probably also to a degree the behavior of other animals — that is somewhat analogous to physical indeterminacy. Just as one cannot set about determining the position and motion of a small particle without upsetting its position and motion, so one cannot experiment with the private worlds of living organisms without significantly altering them. The point is obvious enough: one cannot examine what is going on in the self without the examination's being a new experience, enlarging and changing the self that is under observation.

I ran into an extraordinary instance of this some years ago. As I recall the National Research Council had shortly before issued a report on the wonders of microfilm. Soon after, complaints began to arrive that persons reading microfilm got headaches. Never at a loss, the National Research Council set up the Committee on Visual Fatigue in the Reading of Microfilm. About twenty or thirty of us, supposedly experts either in vision or in fatigue, were brought to Washington for a three-day meeting. Early in the first day it came out that no one present had much idea what visual fatigue is, much less what to do about it. Stranger still, no one seemed to have a much better notion of what fatigue in general might be. Each of us made a speech, but in almost every case it was about something else. I made a speech too, of course about something else. The word "fatigue" was almost never mentioned.

That experience taught me something that may surprise you. There is nothing esoteric about fatigue. It is one of the most ordinary and familiar experiences we have. All of us get tired, and think we know what we mean when we say so. Nothing could seem simpler than to define and test that ordinary condition.

I learned at that meeting that the best and almost the only way to tell whether someone is tired is to ask him. So far as I know, there is even now almost nothing in the realm of science that you can do to verify that statement. I am not speaking here of the fatigue that comes from running a hundred-yard dash; that is just lactic acid in the blood and muscles. I am talking about why one is tired after, say, eight hours of desk work. At Harvard University we used to have an institution called The

Fatigue Laboratory. Shortly before it was disbanded, its director, Bruce Dill, wrote a review on industrial fatigue, which concluded, as I recall, that that kind of fatigue is largely boredom; for a person fatigued by eight hours work of one sort or another can be suddenly resuscitated by being given the chance to dance all night.

That conference in Washington was a frustrating experience for me. At the very end, because he had insisted that it be there, a psychologist gave his paper. He explained that he had prepared a battery of perhaps a dozen searching psychological tests, and had then set about fatiguing people by keeping them awake and busy for as long as seventy-two hours at a stretch. He assured us that there was no doubt whatever that these people were tired. At one sign of that, some of them got to be very irritable, so much so that he sometimes had to send his secretary out of the room. Yet even after seventy-two hours of this, the entire battery of tests revealed no significant changes. The point seemed to be that the process of testing created a new situation that dispelled the fatigue. Just as the interaction with a probing photon upsets the state of an electron, so the interaction with an observer may upset the state of a human subject. Any invasion of the private world of the self is a new experience; one cannot examine the self without significantly altering it.

I should like finally to enter upon highly controversial ground. We have heard lately from various quarters suggestions of enterprises, under scientific auspices I am sorry to say, that though entirely idealistic in intent, could have the effect of a drastic attack upon the small yet precious area of free will. I think of two lines of such development. One is still only potential, not likely to be put into effect soon if indeed ever. It involves the possibility that in the near future it may become possible to control human heredity, to bring this hitherto unpredictable, anarchical, and disorderly process within clean-cut technological control.

One way in which it is proposed to set about this involves so-called test-tube babies. Test-tube babies are a distinct technical possibility; my friend Gregory Pincus produced rabbits in this way about twenty-five years ago. Indeed Pincus did something much more startling, in that he produced his rabbits from eggs that had never been fertilized but had been activated to develop through the manipulations of removing them from a female.[6] Such a test-tube rabbit is not really produced in a test-tube. It is started off in a test-tube and then implanted at an early stage of development in the uterus of another female who acts as foster mother and eventually bears a baby rabbit that is not hers at all, having no genetic connection with her. In principle, probably in fact, one could bring this feat off with human beings, or the much easier enterprise of fertilizing a human egg with sperm outside the body and implanting the early embryo in a foster mother, who would bring it to term. Heaven forfend that such a device were used to speed up the production of human beings. The tried and true methods are already producing too many. One might, however, achieve something else in this way that one could not otherwise, and that is controlled human mating. One could mix just the sperm and just the eggs one wanted.

What would be achieved in that way? In fact it is something rather familiar: breeding by specification. One would have abandoned natural selection for the technological process that Darwin characterized as artificial selection; one would have exchanged the process of organic design for technological design. This is the process by which we have made all our domestic animals; and applied to men, it could yield domesticated men. We have bred domestic animals over many generations of controlled mating to be just what we want of them — the pigs to be fat, the cows to give a lot of milk, the work horses to be heavy and strong, and all of them to be stupid — all, that is, that we use rather than merely patronize as pets. Stupidity and do-

[6] G. Pincus, "The Development of Fertilized and Artificially Activated Rabbit Eggs," *Journal of Experimental Zoology*, LXXXII (1939), 89; "The Breeding of Some Rabbits Produced by Recipients of Artificially Activated Ova," *Proceedings of the National Academy of Sciences*, XXV (1939), 557.

cility are among the traits selected for first of all, for a clever or willful animal can make a lot of trouble.

A closely related type of proposal comes out of the present euphoria with molecular genetics. This is the thought that shortly we may be able to modify either genetic composition or genetic action and so control inheritance by direct chemical intervention.

Both types of enterprise, however benign in intent, have the quality of substituting technology for what have been organic processes and so making determinate and predictable what have so far been indeterminate and beyond our control. As such, they would constitute important inroads, if ever they were allowed to happen, upon the area of unpredictability which I equate with free will.

Another type of development poses a more serious threat, because more immediate, indeed already to a degree in being. This is an attack not upon the unpredictability of our heredity but upon the unpredictability of our history, our accumulation of experience. It proposes to replace our present habits of allowing limited realms of human experience to develop rather haphazardly by conditioning to produce exactly the kinds of behavior one thinks proper.

I once took part in a conversation with a group of other scientists that was going to be chopped up into radio broadcasts. Sitting next to me was a colleague from the Psychology Department. At a certain point he said, "We have the techniques now for producing any kind of human behavior you like. Just give us the specifications, and we will make the men." "Not if I can shoot you first," I said. That seemed to irritate him a little; and then he said something remarkable that I have always remembered. He said: "The chemists have had their chance; the physicists have had their chance; why can't we have our chance?" The only thing I could think to reply was that chemists and physicists work with molecules, and we are willing to deal with molecules statistically; but we insist upon dealing with persons individually. I think that is really the point.

44

Conditioning is designed experience. It substitutes for unplanned and individual experience, and the unpredictability of behavior contingent upon it, a standardized experience that yields dependable behavior. That is its purpose. We already have a lot of it, in home training, schooling, and religious and political ritual. Conceivably there should be more; but the more of that, the less free will.

I had another such experience with a colleague from our Psychology Department. I sat as a member of a horrified audience while he told us how two of his students had created an art lover. They had a roommate, a wholesome, mesomorphic type, who had no interest whatever in art. They decided to apply the methods they had learned from our speaker to turn this athlete into an art lover; and that's what they did, very tidily. They hung a number of pictures about the walls. Knowing that their victim liked attention, they saw to it that for a while he didn't get any. They ignored him utterly, unless by chance his eye happened to light upon a picture; whereupon both roommates would drop everything else and jabber at him excitedly until he turned away. Within a week this chap was looking at pictures all the time and had even begun to talk about them. His roommates felt they had achieved the ultimate triumph when one Sunday morning the athlete rolled over in bed and said, "Hey, fellows, how about going to the museum?" Then they told our speaker, and he told us, with some approval, for I think his point was, don't we want art lovers? — and I think the answer is yes, but not produced in that way.

I think that intuitively we tend to recognize the equation of free will with unpredictability. This manufacture of an art lover raises a problem much like the problem of authenticity in art. I have been in a number of conversations involving the fake Vermeers painted by the Dutch artist, Van Meegeren. Persons who, incidentally, don't seem to me seriously committed to art, have said to me, why care whether a picture is a fake Vermeer if it is beautiful, if it can fool even museum directors? What difference does it make?

An interesting question, and you will have your own notions

about it. For myself, I think the point is that the most that Van Meegeren can do, if he is capable of painting a beautiful picture, is to paint a beautiful Van Meegeren; but he cannot paint any kind of Vermeer. Similarly, that art lover: he was not an art lover in his own right at all; he was a fake, a spurious construction of the persons who designed him. Love of art, if it entered this situation at all, was in the conditioners and merely projected upon their innocent technological product.

Experience that is private and authentic, breeding behavior that is unpredictable and in that sense free, has something of the novelty, the emergent and creative quality of art. It is indeed the source of art. To degrade that free expression to the level of designed and automatic response deprives it of all interest, and all esthetic and moral value. It makes of experience a thing, perhaps useful, but then only as manufactured products are useful.

In sum, I think that we have freedom of will and that it comes out of our uniqueness as individuals, perhaps wholly determined, yet to some degree unpredictable. However limited in scope, it is one of our most precious possessions. As such we should seek to enlarge it; yet that is not the direction in which we are going. On the contrary, many aspects of modern life threaten to erode it; and much that we are offered in the guise of future progress would tend to do the same.

Free will is often inefficient, often inconvenient, and always undependable. That is the character of freedom. We value it in men; we disparage it in machines and in domestic animals. Our technology has given us dependable machines and livestock; we shall have to choose whether to turn it now to giving us more efficient, convenient and reliable men, yet at the cost of our freedom. We had better decide now, for we are already not as free as once we were, and we can lose piecemeal and from within what we would be quick to defend from a frank attack from without. Valuing free will as we do, it is important to come to understand it better, so better to defend and preserve it.

3

THE SCIENCE OF SCIENCE

by Derek J. de Solla Price

If there be some special heaven reserved for historians, or even perhaps some deliciously appropriate hell, I suppose it would be a place of broken idols. It would be a place where material evidence would be readily available to prove beyond all doubt that every popular story was false. Paul Revere did not ride at midnight, Washington had no cherry tree and Hannibal no elephants, Nero never fiddled, and the stories you are liable to read in the Bible would all be necessarily false.

Whatever the uses of historical scholarship are (and much has been written about this topic), there would be little of it, in spite of the need for teachers of the young, if it were not for the special motivation that drives historians. Much of that motivation, it seems to me, is the desire to dig deeper and find out why and how things happened the way they did. In the course of this digging, they always hope for buried treasure — and the nature of that treasure is a new revealed truth showing that the deep reason for things' happening as they did is vastly different from the popular and naïve notion, so well illustrated by the popular stories of this kind, which we have all learned or half heard in our schooldays.

Perhaps the greatest revelation to me in my professional odyssey from physicist to historian of science was the discovery that research in the two subjects felt much the same from inside. The desire of the physicist to achieve some great new understanding

DEREK J. DE SOLLA PRICE is Avalon Professor of the History of Science at Yale University.

of the universe matches that of the historian to comprehend the workings of our society, and the lust for idol-breaking is quite similar. Most striking of all, in the history of science there seems to be a particularly high incidence of fragile idols, of popular stories illustrating a conventional wisdom about science, and this wisdom is soon found to be but a thin coat of wise varnish overlaying an accretion of naïve superstition and half-truth.

As a physicist I had known full well and instinctively about such things as the objectivity of scientists, the relation between experiment and theory, the role of mathematics in physical theory, and the relation between pure science and applied technology, and from my teachers and peers I had quickly learned the social mechanism of how one tried to get there first with the most. As a historian of science, however, it soon became evident to me that in most of these things I had only a partial knowledge and in many I had picked up the wrong end of the stick. For example, Copernicus, as it turns out, did not have a more accurate and economical planetary theory than his predecessors but merely one which though partially true should have been (and was) unacceptable at the time to any good scientist. Galileo almost certainly did not make an experiment from the tower of Pisa, and as a non-mathematical and rather medieval mechanician and popular expositor of physical principles, he did not need to. Though the scientific revolution of the seventeenth century is said to have depended on the new experimental instruments, it becomes clear that the main role of instruments was not the making of better observations, and it was not until long after this period that scientists learned the difficult art of *not* fudging their experimental readings.

More broken idols abound when one looks at the biographies of individual scientists and at their priority disputes. One discovers that the genesis of new ideas deviates far from the tradition of objectivity and impersonality and comes rather by way of highly subjective elements in each man; and that the acceptance or rejection of such ideas is more often than not surrounded by issues of personality of the individual and of his peers. Still more idols break at a touch when one first looks at the history of technology and sees it so different in its methodology and structure from the history of science itself. The case histories show, and the whole historical pattern shows even more clearly, that technology cannot be anything so simple as the application of new scientific knowledge to the mastery of nature and the good of nations.

One cannot long live with thoughts such as these without coming to the inevitable conclusion that our knowledge about modern science may be just as much beset by naïvete and misunderstanding, half-truth and whole error, as is our knowledge about past science. Indeed, in recent years there has been a remarkable reinforcement of such suspicions because of the spilling over and cross-fertilization of new findings from sociology and psychology into the history of science and because of the vital new growth of radical ideas, such as those of Kuhn and Agassi, in the historiography of science. These new contributions begin to give us an "inner theory," a theory that takes what were previously merely the empirical generalizations of historians about the past and raises these generalizations to a new level where we can see that, unless radical changes occur, things must necessarily happen in much the same way in the present and in the future as they did in the past.

What is particularly intriguing about this new knowledge of the history of science, as against economic or social history, or indeed, as against much of the rest of intellectual history, is that science seems in many ways to be universal in space and time, supranational and suprasocietal, so that its behavior appears to be determined by the nature of science itself much more than by the properties of the society in which it is immersed or the desires and aspirations of the men who are its agents or its patrons. It is not, of course, entirely so, but this characteristic appears so strongly that it gives to the history of science a universal currency and a mechanistic determination that can be upsetting and profoundly disturbing to the political or social historian who has become accustomed to finding the fate of a whole civilization dependent on the length of Cleo-patra's nose or on the private aspirations of a Napoleon.

From this personal mixture of iconoclasm and of acquaint-ance with a new and rapidly growing branch of scholarship, I must approach modern science with a mixture of doubt and hope about its analysis. On the one hand, I have grave doubts about the accuracy of our knowledge of the way in which science behaves, develops, and interacts with society; even the most able practitioners of science must surely be misled by many of the myths and idols. On the other hand, I believe that one can effectively pursue hard knowledge in this area and that such knowledge might have a rather attractive and pro-voking universal validity.

Yet to all this I must adduce the paradox that the new knowl-edge about modern science seems to be growing in the midst of strong resistance from both within and without the field of the history of science. The resistance from outside is from scien-tists themselves and is traditional. It has always been part of the special mystique of the scientist that he and he alone can really know about science. Only an esteemed and successful cre-ative scientist can speak for his peers, criticize the state of sci-ence, counsel governments and universities, and guide the policies of laboratories and learned societies. An outsider must be presumed ignorant, not merely of the technical facts, but also of that special knowledge of the life of science that can only be won on its battlefields. This is in spite of the fact that creative artists have their competent art critics who may never have drawn or painted, and that practicing musicians are judged by music critics who cannot play an instrument but who wield nonetheless a pen that contributes much to the progress of their creative industry. Similarly, we have whole legions of teachers of English at schools and universities, communicating the appreciation and criticism of literature because it is part of our culture, not primarily because such teaching may also produce novelists, poets, and essayists. In science, on the other hand, we have had until recently science teaching that was directed only toward the attainment of competence in science rather than toward an appreciation of it. An even better example for contrast is the now accepted scholarship of economics, in which the scholar tries to analyze all that has to do with the production and distribution of a society's goods and assets. We do not demand of a professor of economics that he be first a good and successful businessman, and it is not even claimed that a good grounding in economics will make him a better businessman. But we do recognize that this subject of study is a most important aspect of our society and therefore that it is a fit and proper subject of scholarly curiosity. We recognize, moreover, that it is also a useful trade that may be quite important in deciding the fiscal policy of the nation and preventing the economic evils that attended society in the bad old days when we had only the advice of good businessmen. In science there has been no analogous situation. Perhaps science has a far deeper mystique than business. Every man has some sort of economic life; but without professional qualification in science, one is automatically debarred from knowledge of it except through the diluting processes of popularization and the impact of technologies on our daily lives.

In any case, there is a traditional resistance by scientists to any discussion of science by would-be critics from outside. But even among the men in such fields as the history of science and its sociology, where such criticism is being pursued, there is also another sort of resistance to the analysis of current science. With the true scholarly syndrome, most of my colleagues have as their purposes such things as the establishment and understanding of ancient scientific texts, the working out of what it actually was that Faraday or Ohm achieved, or the circumstances in which quantum mechanics had its genesis, or the way in which the Royal Society was founded by a certain class of men in certain circumstances. We in the history of science have been far too busy winning basic facts and understanding to proceed to any further presumption in setting ourselves up as critics or commentators or analysts of modern science.

Yet in spite of all this internal and external resistance, perhaps even because of it, there has been growing steadily for some decades the sort of criticism and analysis that I have characterized as an analogue of economics but have not yet described. Some such scholarship is quite ancient; Hellenistic and medieval authors wrote interesting and analytical essays about science, and Francis Bacon may best be considered as a pioneer sociologist of science rather than as a scientist himself. The first big push of the recent development came, however, in the late 1920's and early 1930's. So far as I can diagnose its genesis — as an amateur historian of the history of science! — it came about largely through the efforts of predominantly left-wing scientists, roused to a new level of political consciousness through the postrevolutionary development of the Soviet Union. This was a country where communism meant "socialism plus electrification" together with all the other aspects of a nascent science-based educational system and a technology-based economy. It began to be evident that science was not just a part of culture and that technology was not just a matter of inventiveness and industrialization. Science and technology graduated from a sort of sugar-frosting on the cake, from a condiment of civilization, to some vital part of the cake itself, a vitamin in the diet of society.

In this context there arose the famous "planning of Science" debates and the equally famous "Freedom in Science" opposition to them, in which several of the vital issues began to be thrashed out. I find it particularly interesting that although the discussions were plainly party-political, sharply divided by left and right, the most notable and effective protagonists on both sides — Bernal to the left, Baker to the right, for example — were quick to dig deep into what little professional history of science there was and into such sociology and psychology and economics of it as then existed, to provide ammunition for their big guns. It was also at this time that the term "Science of Science" was first proposed by the Ossowskis in a little article in a Polish journal.

Just as it was raging most intensely, this battle was quieted by the coming of World War II. There is no need to underline the dramatic way in which the forces of science and technology erupted into public consciousness through their part in the war. The bomb, missiles, and radar were the overriding forces of military might. Suddenly the comic-strip character of Superman changed from an all-American football player into an equally all-American nuclear physicist. By the end of the war a scientist did not have to have political motivation to be conscious of the social relations of science. As Oppenheimer has said, the physicist had come to know original sin. By the end of the war this country had a huge supply of active scientific manpower that had somehow to be returned to a more or less civilian occupation in a land that now set a high value upon such competence but that had few facilities for hiring it outside the universities, which had only limited employment capabilities.

Thus it came about in the postwar years that willy-nilly, all arguments for planning and freedom notwithstanding, governmental action had to be taken to make funds available for science in the universities and outside; and there was a general realization, both in government and in the body of scientists, that science should be promoted for the good of society and the nation. Augmented by the shock of Sputnik, the tide ran high; but even earlier Washington (and Moscow) had begun to fill with administrators and experts charged with the task of building and maintaining this burgeoning effort in science and technology.

Two important things have happened in the nearly twenty years during which this process has continued. In the first place — in a conclusion curiously agreed upon by both East and West — science has become a direct productive force in society. It had already graduated from a condiment to a vitamin; now it has become the very meat and potatoes of our diet. In the second place, the twenty years have brought about a new expertise in how science and technology are in practice to be administered and nourished for the purposes of society.

Many of the processes of decision-making have still to be

played by ear and many involve no deeper knowledge than the administration of anything else, but nevertheless in the course of this experience, there seems to have begun all over the world some generation and consolidation of a conventional wisdom about the ways in which science policy can operate and the ways it cannot. Some parts of this wisdom are built on trial and error, other parts are empirical generalizations, and others are based upon pieces of research which have been undertaken, often on an in-house basis, by government departments or industrial organizations to find out how best to do what they wish. But slowly there has been coming into being a corpus of expert knowledge about the organization and behavior of science which is such that it now has to be learned the hard way by any person coming into the business. It can no longer, in many areas, be absorbed by the gentle process of osmosis, and this is beginning to make it particularly tough for the eminent scientist who is kicked upstairs to a post of high responsibility in administration and decision-making.

Attending this accumulation of a body of expert knowledge about the administration of science, with all its growing sophistication and consolidation into a full-time occupation for a strong man, there has begun during the last few years a most exciting new development. The first few steps have been taken in bringing this body of knowledge into direct relation with those disinterested fields of scholarship that have studied science and scientists from the viewpoints of the historian, the sociologist, the psychologist, and the economist. I feel we have here a very rich area of cross-fertilization between the fields of scholarship severally and between each of them and the relevant areas of expert organizational knowledge that we have acquired and that we still need for practical purposes. Gradually each part of the complex is coming out of the isolation of its original matrix in a conventional academic discipline or area of administrative expertise, and these parts are beginning visibly to feed on each other so as to give birth to a single discipline. It is this infant or embryonic discipline that has already

54

been dubbed the "Science of Science" — though even those of us who have heard it for a few years and measured its repetitions against the name of Galileo Galilei still cavil at the term and hope it will not turn out to be as phoney as it sounds at first. We also feel it may be quite a long time before it welds itself together into a single discipline instead of the several splinters and *ad hoc* investigations of which it is now constituted. Perhaps it should be admitted to the scholastic catalog only as several sciences of science, and perhaps several humanities of science, too.

The present state of the Science of Science consists then of a stratum of knowledge that is being explored in two directions — from the top and from the bottom. From the top we have the administrators and experts on science policy who are forever exploring new areas and digging deeper to base their findings on a suitable foundation. From the bottom we have those who are starting from historical analyses and the sociological and psychological characteristics of scientists and gradually building a picture of the way in which science and scientists work in various circumstances. Somewhere in between there are economists and gatherers of statistical data who reach out to theoretical bases below and to the stock-in-trade of the administrator above.

Such analyses as we have indicate uniformly that the needs for the Science of Science are becoming greater as several old problems are magnified and new crises explode upon us. The increasing importance of science in society is matched only by the rate at which its costs grow and the extent to which it is dominating the lives of more people and better people in more and more countries. It seems to me, therefore, that we have an urgent need to force the development of this new discipline, to nourish its component parts and to bring them to bear on present needs.

I have tried to describe the genesis and the motivation of this new and embryonic science, in which the tools of the scientist are to be turned upon science itself both to satisfy our inner

55

curiosity about it and to provide a social technology by which science might be manipulated by society to satisfy its ends. But now, in a spirit of intense curiosity and urgent need, I shall attempt a task never hitherto expressly formulated. To help and to provoke my growing band of colleagues in this area, I should like to try to provide a program of research — achieved, in progress, and yet to be attempted — that would draw together most of what we know about science and make it available as a foundation for decision-making. At the beginning I must make the caveat that any program I draw up will of course be biased by my own interests and limited by my ignorance of many results already available; I can only hope that others will come forward with correctives and that the provocation may lead more people into this important and clearly underdeveloped area.

As elsewhere within science the initial problems are inevitably those of methodology and concepts. As for the methodology, again as in many other sciences, it seems to me inevitable that we should choose as a matrix for the subject a quantitative rather than a qualitative approach. This is dictated by the fact that we have already available a large corpus of numerical information about manpower, money, publications, and institutions, information which bears directly on many of the interesting and important current issues. Furthermore, many of the needs in administration are for quantitative decisions — for example, in the allocation of resources to several competing claimants — rather than yes/no decisions. Lastly, it is well known that one can often proceed from a quantitative treatment or model to a qualitative one but only with great difficulty in the opposite direction. Thus we can begin with a numerical analysis and draw from that a set of models and theories that will link with the qualitative portions of our treatment. In particular, a statistical analysis of science can provide a matrix, and we can then look for pegs on which to hang the further findings of historians, sociologists, and other investigators.

If the methodology is to be quantitative, the conceptual models and definitions must be chosen with that purpose in mind. The situation is such that our first choice of concept or definition will entail many others and set the pattern of the matrix simply because of compatibility — each part must fit with every other. There is therefore considerable importance to be attached to the quantitative starting point. Again, there is little free choice; this starting point must be a delimitation of the universe to be considered — we must find a quantifying definition for science as distinct from non-science. Although a journey of a thousand leagues begins with but a single step, this step is always the most difficult, and the first step here is no exception, in spite of the fact that multitudes of authors since Francis Bacon must have begun their deliberations with a definition of science. To say that science consists of the aggregate of chemistry, physics, biology, and so on, merely begs the question, for we must then separately define these subjects — and also decide whether mathematics, sociology, political science, Egyptology, and other fields are to be counted in or out. Similarly, all the substantive properties of science analyzed in the philosophy of science are of little avail here, for although in principle some of the ideas of logical networks of theories, propositions, and so on, might be made quantitative I know of no reasonable success in achieving numerical results.

To begin with, then, I shall take as an operational definition of science something that can act as a peg for a good deal of the work of sociologists and historians and something about which a good store of quantitative information is readily available. All historians must take as their point of departure the prime documents in the case; for historians of science this means the scientific papers in learned journals and the books in which science is published. In the sociology of science, as well, the matter of publication has been a central theme in the consideration of the institutions by which private intellectual property is created and maintained — and sometimes quarreled about in priority disputes. A great deal of work has been done in digging deeper than the formal publications, in finding out, for example, the informal communication processes preceding publication and in determining the relation between what actually went on and what is reported in the literature. Nevertheless, the scientific publication — or report — represents in a sense an end product of science and a fixed point in any discussions.

To the scientist himself, the publication represents some mysteriously powerful, eternal, and open archive of the Literature into which he is reading his findings. Only in very rare and special instances does one have to consider pure scientific work in which there is no end product of literature. These would include pathological cases such as that of Henry Cavendish, who researched diligently but did not publish the bulk of his finding, which were therefore lost for a century until they were disinterred by Clerk Maxwell only a few years after the valuable results had been discovered independently by others. Is unpublished work like this, or work that is suppressed and unpublished because it is a national secret, a contribution to science? I find, in general, that it is fair enough to say it is not. Science is not science that communication lacks! In some ways it is a little hard to lose Cavendish from the ranks of contributing scientists and to admit no contribution either from the unpublished researches of Leonardo da Vinci, but on the whole it seems just. A more serious, but rather useful, consequence is that this usage immediately distinguishes science from a great deal of that technology in which the end product may involve no publications (or only secret ones) but only a new product or process or a portion of a process that may not even be recorded separately in a patent.

Our definition holds, then, that science is that which is published in scientific journals, papers, reports, and books. In short, it is that which is embodied in the Literature. Conveniently enough, this Literature is far easier to define, delimit, and count than anything else one might deal with. Because of its central function for scientists, it has been subjected to centuries of systematization by indexes, classifications, journals of abstracts, and retrieval systems. By far the greater part of the Literature is now or has at one time been on the research front — we might distinguish this as "Research Literature." Only a lesser part consists of summaries, surveys, and other boiling-downs, such as textbooks and popular treatises. All such literature can be, and in very many cases has actually been, counted, classified, and followed through the years as a time series. The chief component of the Research Literature, for example, can be defined as the papers published in the scientific serials included in the *World List of Scientific Periodicals* — a familiar tool of all reference librarians. It is true that this list duplicates many scholarly journals that include some scientific papers, but clearly it cannot be expected to list those that erupt with only one such paper in a century.

But with such a first step taken, quantitative results begin to emerge quite readily. We know, to a first approximation, that the number of science journals has been growing steadily since the inception of modern science in the seventeenth century at a rate of 5 per cent per annum compound interest. This gives a doubling every fifteen years, a factor of ten every thirty years, and a factor of about one hundred thousand since the effective beginning *ca.* 1700. We know, too, that journals have a very high mortality rate, so that for every three that have been born, two have died and only one now survives — the current list of journals therefore consists of only about thirty-five thousand in the world. In fact we know even more about this mortality; for every journal living about one hundred years, there are one hundred journals living only one year each, fifty living two years, ten living ten years and so on. For an illustration of the consequence of these figures, let us suppose first that all bound annual volumes of all periodicals were the same size. The whole library would then contain one hundred thousand titles, running from a single volume to a run of more than two hundred fifty for the oldest. Half of this library would then be contained in only about three hundred journals, each of which had a run greater than about fifteen years; but for this year's new additions the library would have thirty-five thousand vol-

umes, each from a different journal. The high mortality therefore leaves a small core of tried and tested, long-lived journals that carry a high proportion of the literature. Outside this
core is an almost open-ended community of lesser journals,
important in any one year but contributing less and less to the
total archive.

To get this result we have made the unwarranted assumption
that all annual volumes of periodicals are the same size, which,
of course, they are not. The distribution is a quite regular log-
normal one; that is to say, the logarithms of the sizes in numbers of papers per year are distributed on a normal curve
about a mean that grows only slowly with time. Now it happens that there is a good correlation between the ages of the
journals and their sizes, and probably their prestige and importance, too. Thus the oldest journals that form our core are
also, in general, the biggest and the most important, and hence
the core will contain much more than half the literature in numbers of papers and even more than this if we load the core by
any reasonable measure of worthiness. To jump ahead a little,
the core phenomenon is such that if one starts from the very
tiny group of journals, papers, projects, or men that account
for something more than half the total effort and proceeds out-
ward into the almost infinite general population, one gets only
a small percentage increase in value, say about 10 per cent to
start with, for each doubling of the population. This is why total lists, of all American scientists, or all the world's journals
are so huge, though everyone knows that the periodicals and
people that really matter are quite few in number.

Returning now to the main thread, we must overcome the
difficulty that the statistical treatment so far has depended on
an arbitrary selection of journals by the world list. This can be
converted in the following fashion to an objective method that
tells much more. There is now just beginning to be available
a new device called the *Science Citation Index*. This takes the
papers appearing in about one thousand of the most important
journals of the world, in all fields of science, and lists by author

all the papers and other sources cited in the bibliographies and footnotes of each of the original papers. If you are interested in a certain field, this index, when properly used, will tell you what material was published last year which cites earlier papers by you or your colleagues. You look up these papers directly in the index and see what new papers are citing this previous work. Thus there is a bibliographic tool that can go forward in time, rather than only backward, as in old-style bibliography hunting.

Now it is possible to use this citation index statistically for our purposes, quite apart from the practical use it may have for scientists and librarians. Even if we agree that many of the citations in papers may be purely decorative, put in for historical or personal reasons and so on, it is plain that their statistical behavior in the large is regular and meaningful. One can, for example, start with each journal on the list and tabulate the other journals that it cites and also the journals that cite it; these lists may then be set in rank order, or a total matrix may be established showing how each journal fits with its neighbors. Note that results of this kind are largely independent of the original choice of journals for indexing. Even if *Physical Review*, say, had been omitted from the sources, as soon as the citations from a few other journals publishing physics papers had been analyzed, it would be obvious that *Physical Review* was for all of them a most important sector of all citations. Likewise, if we consider the numbers of papers available in each journal to provide citations and the number available to be cited, it will appear that some journals clump together in a "mutually-citing population," whereas other journals and clumps are far from this group. These clumps, each consisting of a central core surrounded by a diffuse body of lesser literature, correspond roughly to the separate disciplines of science. In principle, I believe, they could be mapped, with hybrid subjects like physical chemistry and chemical physics occupying the borderlands between the big areas of physics and chemistry.

Not only could such a map be drawn quite objectively, but

its changing pattern could be followed through the years so as to show the activity bursting out here and dying there as fields come into being, increase or decrease their production of papers, or die completely. As an interesting outcome of such a mapping, I think one would find a quite large class of allegedly scientific journals that do not appear at all or appear only on the far periphery of some of the clumps. That is to say, there seem to be journals that do not cite other journals much, and are not in turn much cited. I would compare these in their function to newspapers, each reflecting the world's events rather than consuming the products of other newspapers and being consumed in their turn. To such a genus belongs quite a lot of the literature that one might classify as engineering, or clinical medicine, or data reporting. I do not quite understand the genesis of this growing but non-cumulative literature, but it seems to be some epiphenomenon of science, if it is science at all. At all events, one has now, in principle, a way of deciding objectively what literature is part of the cumulation of science, how it is divided by scientific sectors, and how it grows at its various rates. By sampling a fair population from all sectors or from any one sector, we can determine statistically the breakdown by country of publication, by language, and so on. We even have some trial investigations that show, for the United States in particular, the source of funds supporting the research that is published and the way in which this support changed with time in the critical period when federal funds were beginning to replace private and university support (without, as it happens, altering the growth rate of publication in the fields considered.)

An interesting point now arises. If we examine the breakdowns by country and by field, it appears that most countries have amounts of the various sciences in proportion to the sizes of these scientific fields and to their own total scientific size. What is going on if significant deviations from this total picture are found? — if physics, for example, on the world scale is 15 per cent of the total scientific effort but in the United States is 30 per cent? I think there would be a good case for saying that this would be wrong policy for the United States and uneconomic unless some positive reason could be produced to the contrary. Physics research is universal, and an overcontribution by one country would be adding more to the world total than could be drawn out as new developments on the research front; and the money and support could be better utilized, therefore, by adding to the other relatively neglected sciences in proportion to their sizes in the world scientific market. Thus, I think we can arrive at a position from which in principle the policies for support of the basic sciences may be objectively handled and their funding suitably proportioned for those areas where one does not wish willfully to disturb an evident status quo.

Having established an objective monitoring of the literature, we may proceed to problems of scientific manpower. Here again, the vital first step is one of concepts and definitions. For the same reason as before, that of ease in quantification, it now becomes strategic to define a scientist in terms of the literature. The easiest line is to say that we shall consider a person to be a scientist if at any time in his life he has authored (or perhaps even co-authored) a paper in one of the scientific journals that we have already defined and classified in principle. Again, in principle, there is little difficulty in showing that there is a mortality pattern in productivity which is relatively constant from country to country, from field to field, and even rather spectacularly constant with time, so that it has scarcely changed in two or three centuries. The natural distribution of productivities, and perhaps even degrees of goodness and competence, here again follows something like the log-normal curve that one would expect if scientific talent were distributed through the population in the same way as the heights of men, or their wealth, or anything else. Further, there is the high mortality rate for individual scientific production, like that already found in journals. This mortality pattern shows us that for every three people once pulled into the research front about two have been excreted from it, presumably into activities that do not cumulate literature, activities like teaching, administration, and the production of new goods and processes, as well as completely non-scientific activities. In short, it can be seen that in principle, if we know the volume of literature in any field and country and time, we can compute the number of minimal scientists defined by this literature and also the number of those with any higher degree of productivity. In particular we can, if we wish, compute the number of "core scientists" who are responsible for half the volume of the work and more than half of the important work; and we can also determine what number of new scientists must be brought up to the point of publishing a single paper in order to maintain this scientific population and enable it to grow at the rate prescribed by the world total.

Once we have shown that there is this kind of watertight and objective scheme whereby scientific literature and manpower may be measured and related, we may expand the study in several directions. First, we can take account of the large corpus of non-ideal definitions and investigations that have already been made and relate them to this quantitative corpus, thereby extending the results in a very rich and practical way. Second, we can consider the various statistical regularities that have been found empirically and inquire why they have the particular forms observed. In many cases, we can even now begin to see certain underlying laws and principles that have a deep and obvious validity. It seems likely that this sort of consideration will soon raise whole areas of investigation from the level of empirical generalizations, like Kepler's Laws, to the level of laws which necessarily hold by virtue of basic principles, like Newton's Laws of Motion. Lastly, of course, the now well-integrated central corpus can be extended and deepened to link with historical and sociological studies, on the one hand, and with the ramifications of science policy discussions, on the other. I shall give a few selected samples of possible extensions of the central corpus in these three different ways.

With respect to the first point, it is interesting to see the use we can make even of imperfect data. Even though we have no over-all map of the clumps of journals on a field-by-field basis, we do have measurements for several of the most important journals in various fields that give the incidence of the numbers of authors per paper and the number of references per paper. From this data it is quite clear that there is a field-by-field variation. A surprising aspect of multiple authorship is that its remarkable growth in some areas, such as physics, began long before the introduction of "big machines" and the teams that are required to carry out experiments with them. This finding leads one to suppose, that in such a field, papers with twenty-seven authors might well be regarded as a means of communication between the people involved and as a mean of securing publications for persons who would otherwise be only minimal producers, so that in these circumstances, the big machine is perhaps more the occasion for the multiplicity than its cause. Further, from the pattern of the numbers of citations contained by various papers, it would appear that some areas, notably the technologies and clinical medicine, feed on the previous literature very much less than the norm, having only about five references per paper instead of the norm of fifteen per paper. Does this simply mean that in some subjects there is a different convention about how many papers one should normally cite? I think not. It would appear to me that here we have an indication of an effective difference between fields — that the function of the literature in the fields which cite few sources is not primarily to provide data for other workers at the research front. By our definitions, one arrives at the provoking result that although literature is produced in these fields it is apparently only weakly scientific.

As instances of the more important "Laws of Motion" that might be established in the Science of Science, I would like to consider the one which tells us the nature of distributions in size, quality, and so on, and the one which governs the normal way in which the things that are measured grow with time. In all known instances of the distribution laws, giving the number of authors producing n papers, or the number of institutions producing *n* scientists, one finds the same pattern of extreme inequality that is found for the distribution of sizes of cities within a country or for the distribution of personal incomes in a competitive society. It has already been pointed out by Merton on sociological grounds that in science, part of what happens is accounted for by what he calls the "Matthew principle" — unto him that hath is given — to which we might adduce the complementary negative — from him that hath not, shall be taken even that he hath. To put it another way, we have a regularity similar to the Fechner or Weber law of experimental psychology, in which each increase in effect is due to a constant increase in the ratio of stimulus. The chance that a man will go from his first paper to his second (about one chance in four) is the same as the chance of his going from his second paper to his fourth, from his fourth to his eighth, and so on; and the chance of an institution's growing from ten Ph.D.'s in physics per year to twenty is the same as that of its growing from one hundred to two hundred.

In a normal population one gets, therefore, a random curve of errors, not in the distribution of the measures but rather in their logarithms, and on the whole, this simple model provides a fairly good first approximation to the empirical observations. It is important to note that this is a built-in mechanism of science and that it acts as a sort of cybernetic control over a population. It would be as difficult to make effective a decree establishing throughout the country a thousand equal institutions that would each produce ten science Ph.D.'s a year as it would be to enforce a decision that our huge cities be abolished and replaced by a population uniformly distributed over the map of the country.

Continuing this line of reasoning, we can see that the same laws make it much easier to state the universally found exponential growth of science as a steady and linear growth of the logarithms of our conventional measures of size. Here again, one can dig deeper, using the techniques of citation indexing. In a current project, I have been attempting to see what happens if one looks for the relations, not between different scientific journals but between individual authors. It appears that the entire research front of science may be divided into distinct clumps of authors, each having some one hundred members, give or take a factor of two; and that within each clump the peer group, or "Invisible College," makes its living by taking in each others' washing. The properties of these small clumps are particularly exciting for the social analysis of science and may be of deep significance in practical problems of administering and serving the needs for such groups. What is even more important is that we can begin to see that it is this mechanism for rapid accumulation of research through the interactions within a peer group that distinguishes the progress of science from that of scholarship in general. In fact, it is possible to derive a parameter that measures the extent to which research in a field is growing from immediately previous work rather than drawing on the entire past of derived results. This parameter then gives a measure of where that field of research stands in the spectrum that runs from pure science at one end to pure non-science at the other. Furthermore, one can see that it is this short-range interaction that makes science grow so much faster than non-science; and indeed, one may derive a good approximate value for the growth rate in terms of a simple model of the interaction. It turns out from this that the old knowledge breeds new knowledge at a constant rate so that we have growth at compound interest — a linear growth of the logarithm — as a necessary consequence of the basic situation rather than a mere empirical finding.

Finally, I must turn to a couple of samples of the way in which this new corpus of theory may be extended to meet the feelers being put out by those in urgent need of information and theories for practical planning. My first sample concerns the whole area of economic studies of science, where one is concerned with financial cost and industrial growth. Our new technique gives us a means of estimating, field by field, country by country, the number of people who are engaged at any time in producing the cumulating end product of literature, which, as we have said, constitutes the stuff of scientific knowledge. If we wish, our technique can also tell us the degree of effectiveness with which the cumulation is occurring at any part of the research front or, in greater detail, whether any specific group of researchers is central in a clump or only peripheral. Since we have a measure of the manpower directly involved, by multiplying this number by the average salary or income of men in each sector, we can arrive at the amount of money spent directly in supporting the scientific population. This amount can, of course, be broken down and followed with respect to the years, the source and nature of the funding, or any other variable one wishes. By sampling, we can then add to this, sector by sector, the amount that has been spent on auxiliary services of technicians, secretaries, and assistants, and on buildings, libraries, apparatus, and machinery. When the various amounts are added together, one can get a picture of the total expenditure on pure science, the manpower directly and indirectly involved, and the way in which the over-all pattern agrees or disagrees with the similar profiles for other countries and for the world as a whole.

If we compare these figures with our own national expenditures for research and development, it becomes obvious that in many sectors a great deal of money is being spent that does not result in a corresponding output in cumulating literature and that this money is therefore not purchasing what we have defined as scientific knowledge. This, by and large, is the expenditure that is being made on technology, on the production of new products and processes and services. In this area one is no longer concerned with a universal and international state of knowledge to which every country subscribes but with a set of particular products which are being purchased by our own country for its military power, prestige, medical well-being, or industrial profit. The quantitative separation of the element of technology from scientific knowledge, then, enables us to see a little more clearly just what is being bought and how much is being paid for it. It now becomes possible, for example, to see how much one is paying for space science and how much for a lunar landing or a communications satellite, how much in particle physics and how much in reactor technology as against reactor science. Of course, there is some reciprocal relation between science and technology, field by field, but in the past we have never managed to estimate the dependence accurately because all previous figures have been lumped together in a somewhat confusing fashion.

My final demonstration of the power of this method concerns deviations from the normal and standard exponential growth of science. We now have several key examples that indicate that, although the normal pattern in science is a doubling in size every ten to fifteen years, new fields and new countries emerge by exploding into a vacuum, so to speak, at a much greater rate; whereas old fields and old countries behave as if they are meeting with saturation conditions that make growth considerably slower than the norm. A number of interesting case studies now exist that throw new light on the birth of a field and the inception of science in a newly developing country. We know that there is a rather ill-defined initial phase that consists of the sudden onset of "take-off conditions"; this is followed by a rapid growth to a certain point beyond which normal exponential growth conditions are maintained. In a study of the growth of modern science in late nineteenth-century Japan, it has been shown that the crucial phase occurred with the widespread reform of the educational system and a switch to teaching in Japanese as well as the European languages. Such findings are directly applicable to policy problems of the developing countries today. Perhaps the most provoking result of this Science of Science analysis is found, however, in the possibility of an onset of saturation conditions in some countries, notably the United States and the Soviet Union. It would seem that one of our most pressing problems is going to be that of science in the overdeveloped countries, where difficulties are already being encountered, not only in the supply of high-talent manpower, but in the rapidly increasing costs of utilizing this manpower. Because of this deceleration, we may find the most important scientific countries automatically taking a lesser and lesser place in the world total and therefore being faced with even more difficult choices than they have now as to how to deploy their resources and talents.

So far as I can see, the basic problems of organizing science and technology are increasing so rapidly that we are headed for demands as urgent as those which faced the profession of economics during the financial crises of the great depression. It is with these demands in mind that I urge that we make every effort to develop as rapidly as possible and to have ready some well-integrated and hard theory in the Science of Science.

4

MIND, BRAIN, AND HUMANIST VALUES

by Roger W. Sperry

Science, Antiscience, and Values

As a scientist invited to discuss humanist implications of the brain-behavior sciences, I find myself feeling a little like one who has been asked to mount the stand in self-defense as the accused. As they say back in Grade Two these days, for every action there is an equal and opposing reaction; and the recent sharp boom in science has not come without a corresponding rise in the voices of antiscience. Some of the going complaints in this regard are no doubt familiar: It is not only that science is going to blow us all off the globe, or crowd us off with its programs for death control, but that even the good things resulting from science — the sum total of all the better-things-for-better-living — have failed, we are told, to add substantially to a genuine satisfaction in living. And when it comes to the more profound humanist concerns, the reasons for living and the meaning and the value of it all, science seems only to take away and destroy, they say, and then refuses on principle to answer for its actions or even to be concerned with matters of values.

To some, even the objective explanatory progress that science is supposed to be making toward truth and the great central mystery of the universe begins to look like merely a handy system of humanoid guesses and correlational probabilities with no

---

ROGER W. SPERRY is F. P. Hixon Professor of Psychobiology at the California Institute of Technology.

real verification possible. Others liken our explanatory progress to the penetration of a great maze that gets ever bleaker, the innermost chamber of which, should it ever be reached, being likely to hold exactly nothing or perhaps just the self-reflections of the scientists' own thought processes. And then, about as fast as our comprehension and control of nature goes up, anti-science sees man's rating in the grand design going down.

Before going on, I had better explain that the reference to values above and in the title was not accidental, though I well realize that any mixing of values and science tends to serve as a red flag in some quarters. Some of us may already be wondering, Since when do scientists presume to carry a license for discussions of values? Value judgments, we have all heard, lie outside the realm of science. Value matters are for popes and prophets, for philosophers and perhaps boy scout and YMCA leaders, but not for science or scientists. As a student of brain and behavior, I have never been quite able to accept this. It seems the same as saying that value judgments lie outside the realm of knowledge and understanding. It is like saying that the best method we know of applying the human brain to problems of understanding must be discarded when it comes to problems of values. It is like saying that economics is riding under false colors in the National Science Foundation and ought to be exposed and expelled. And it is like saying that science is able to deal only with those phenomena and products of evolution that appeared prior to the emergence of higher brains, with their wants, needs, goal-directed properties, and, of course, the corresponding value systems that these impose.

Values have natural and logical origins. They are interdependent and interrelated in logical, hierarchical systems. These systems, and the perturbations thereof, ought to be subject to study and analysis and perhaps prediction and even some experimentation on a model basis these days, with computer assistance. I have always wondered whether rather little harm and perhaps much good in the long run might not come from opening to the free winds of scientific skepticism and inquiry even the most revered of our traditional and cultural values.

Humanist Impacts of Behavioral Science

We can now turn to our main question, What have been the major impacts, from the *humanist* standpoint, of the recent developments in the sciences that deal with mind and brain? At first glance the record achieved by the brain-behavior sciences during the past half-century must seem to the humanist to read less like a list of contributions and advancements than like a list of major criminal offenses. The accusations that antiscience can raise in this area are not exactly trivial. For example, before science, man had reason to believe that he possessed a mind that was potent and full of something called "consciousness." Our modern experimental objective psychology and the neurosciences in general would divest the human brain of this fantasy and, in doing so, would dispense not only with the conscious mind but with most of the other spiritual components of human nature, including the immortal soul. Before science, man used to think that he was a spiritually free agent, possessing free will. Science tells us free will is just an illusion and gives us, instead, causal determinism. Where there used to be purpose and meaning in human behavior, science now shows us a complex biophysical machine with positive and negative feedback, composed entirely of material elements, all obeying the inexorable and universal laws of physics and chemistry. Thanks to Freud, with some assistance from astrophysics, science can be accused further of having deprived the thinking man of his Father in heaven, along with heaven itself. Freud's devastating indictment is said by many to have reduced much of man's formalized religion to little more than manifestations of neurosis.

Man's inner self and his heritage have not fared much better. Thanks to Darwin, and to Freud again, man now enters this life, not trailing clouds of glory, as the poet once had it, but trailing instead clouds of jungle-ism and bestiality, full of carnal impulses and a predisposition to Oedipal and other complexes. The confining veneer of our civilization is seen to be superficial, and when it rubs thin or cracks, the animal within quickly shows through. These and related lesser onslaughts on the worth and the meaning of human nature tend to add up, one item reinforcing another, to yield a pretty dim over-all picture that is certainly not heartening to think about — and in science we generally don't think about it. Doubt and rejection of science by humanist thinkers in favor of other roads to truth is not hard to understand; and even for the scientist himself, the picture drawn by science imposes a severe test of his credo that it is better to know the truth, however ugly, and to live in accordance, than to live and die by false premises and illusory values.

But for myself, speaking as a brain researcher — and one not too familiar with matters ethical and philosophical and hence in a position to speak with some conviction — I find myself and my hypothetical working model for the brain to be in marked disagreement with many, if not the majority, of the foregoing implications especially and with that whole general picture of human nature that seems to emerge from the currently prevailing objective, materialistic approach of the brain-behavior sciences. When the humanist is led to favor the implications of modern materialism over the older idealistic values in these and related matters, I suspect that he has been taken, that science has sold society and itself a somewhat questionable bill of goods. There is not space here to present the whole story behind these remarks, and so I will try to concentrate selectively on what would seem to be the centermost issues, hoping that if the central foundation of the materialist view can be undermined the resultant crumbling in the upper structures will become evident.

The Nature of Consciousness: The Central Issue

Most of the disagreements that I have referred to revolve around, or hinge either directly or indirectly upon, a central point of controversy that emerges from the following question: Is it possible, in theory or in principle, to construct a complete, objective explanatory model of brain function without including consciousness in the causal sequence?

If the prevailing view in neuroscience is correct, that consciousness and mental forces in general can be ignored in our objective explanatory model, then we come out with materialism and all its implications. On the contrary, if it turns out that conscious mental forces do in fact govern and direct the nerve-impulse traffic and other biochemical and biophysical events in the brain and, hence, do have to be included as important features in the objective chain of control, then we come out at the opposite pole, or at mentalism, and with quite a different and more idealistic set of values all down the line. We deal here, of course, with the old mind-body dichotomy, the age-old problem of mind versus matter, the issue of the spiritual versus the material, on which books and books have been written and philosophies have foundered ever since man started to think about his inner world and to question its relation to the outer "real" world.

Let us begin by stating the case against consciousness and mind as raised by today's objective experimental psychology, psychobiology, neurophysiology, and the related disciplines. The best way to deal with consciousness or introspective, subjective experience in any form, they tell us, is to ignore it. Inner feelings and thoughts cannot be measured or weighed; they cannot be centrifuged or photographed, chromatographed, spectrographed, or otherwise recorded or dealt with objectively by any scientific methodology. As some kind of introspective, private, inner something, accessible only to the one experiencing individual, they simply must be excluded by policy from any scientific model or scientific explanation.

Furthermore, the neuroscientist of today feels he has a pretty fair idea about the kinds of things that excite and fire the nerve cells of the brain. Cell membrane changes, ion flow, chemical transmitters, pre- and post-synaptic potentials, sodium pump effects and the like, may be on his list of acceptable causal influences — but not consciousness. Consciousness, in the objective approach, is clearly made a second-rate citizen in the causal picture. It is relegated to the inferior status of (*a*) an inconsequential by-product, (*b*) an epiphenomenon (a sort of outsider on the inside), or most commonly, (*c*) just an inner aspect of the one material brain process. Scientists can see the brain as a complex, electrochemical communications network, full of nerve impulse traffic and other causally directed chemical and physical phenomena, with all elements moved by respectable scientific laws of physics, chemistry, physiology, and the like; but few are ready to tolerate an interjection into this causal machinery of any mental or conscious forces.

This is the general stance of modern behavioral science out of which comes today's prevailing objective, mechanistic, materialistic, behavioristic, fatalistic, reductionistic view of the nature of mind and psyche. This kind of thinking is not confined to our laboratories and the classrooms, of course. It leaks and spreads, and though never officially imposed on the societies of the Western world, we nevertheless see the pervasive influence of creeping materialism everywhere we turn.

Once we have materialism squared off against mentalism in this way, I think we must all agree that neither is going to win the match on the basis of direct, factual evidence. The facts simply do not go far enough to provide the answer, or even to come close. Those centermost processes of the brain with which consciousness is presumably associated are simply not understood. They are so far beyond our comprehension at present that no one I know of has been able even to imagine their nature. We are speaking here of the brain code, the physiological language of the cerebral hemispheres. There is good reason to believe that this language is built of nerve impulses and related excitatory effects in nerve cells and fibers and perhaps also in those glia cells that are said to outnumber the nerve cells in the brain by about ten to one. And we would probably be safe in the further noncommittal statement that the brain code is built of spatiotemporal patterns of excitation. But when it comes to even imagining the critical variables in these patterns that correlate with the variables that we know in inner, conscious experience, we are still hopelessly lost.

Furthermore, the central unknowns directly associated with consciousness seem to be rather well cushioned on both the input and output sides of the brain by further zones of physiological unknowns. Our explanatory picture for brain function is reasonably satisfactory for the sensory input pathways and the distal portion of the motor outflow. But that great in-between realm, starting at the stage where the incoming excitatory messages first reach the cortical surface of the brain, still today is very aptly referred to as the "mysterious black box."

To conclude that conscious, mental or psychic, forces have no place in filling this gap in our explanatory picture is at least to go well beyond the facts into the realm of intuition and speculation. The objective, materialist doctrine of behavioral science, which tends to be identified with a rigorous scientific approach, is thus seen to rest, in fact, on an insupportable mental inference that goes far beyond the objective evidence and hence is founded on the cardinal sin of science. One can still find here and there in the literature a modicum of some final, perhaps "last rite," respect paid to the psyche. For example, there is the acceptance by Charles Sherrington of the possible coexistence of two separate phenomenal realms in the brain, and there is the stand of Carl Rogers that man's inner experience must be recognized as well as the brain mechanism of objective psychology. In the existence of two such very different realms, Rogers sees a lasting paradox with which we all must learn to live. But even the dualists are quite prepared to go along these days with the conviction held by most brain researchers — up to some 99.9 per cent of us, I suppose — that conscious mental forces can be safely ignored, insofar as the objective, scientific study of the brain is concerned.

An Alternative Mentalist Position

In the pages that follow, I am going to line myself up with the 0.1 per cent or so mentalist minority in a stand that admittedly also goes well beyond the facts. It is a position, however, that seems to me equally strong and somewhat more appealing than those we have just outlined. In my own hypothetical brain model, conscious awareness does get representation as a very real causal agent and rates an important place in the causal sequence and chain of control in brain events, in which it appears as an active, operational force. Any model or description that leaves out conscious forces, according to this view, is bound to be sadly incomplete and unsatisfactory. The conscious mind in this scheme, far from being put aside as a by-product, epiphenomenon, or inner aspect, is located front and center, directly in the midst of the causal interplay of cerebral mechanisms. Mind and consciousness are put in the driver's seat, as it were: They give the orders, and they push and haul around the physiology and the physical and chemical processes as much as or more than the latter processes direct them. This scheme is one that puts mind back over matter, in a sense, not under or outside or beside it. It is a scheme that idealizes ideas and ideals over physical and chemical interactions, nerve impulse traffic, and DNA. It is a brain model in which conscious mental psychic forces are recognized to be the crowning achievement of some five hundred million years or more of evolution.

Now, what is the argument in favor of mentalism, the argument that holds that ideas and other mental entities push around the physiological and biochemical events in the brain? The argument is simple and goes as follows: First, it contends that mind and consciousness are dynamic, emergent (pattern or configurational) properties of the living brain in action. There are usually plenty of "takers" on this first point, including even some of the tough-minded brain researchers, as, for example, the outstanding neuroanatomist, C. J. Herrick. Second, the argument goes a critical step farther and insists that these emergent properties in the brain have causal potency — just as they do elsewhere in the universe. And there we have the simple answer to the age-old enigma of consciousness. Who was it who said, that nothing is so simple as yesterday's solution, nothing so complicated as tomorrow's problems?

But let us spell out this answer a little further, since this whole subject has at times been a bit complicated. To put it very simply, it comes down to the issue of who pushes whom around in the population of causal forces that occupy the cranium. It is a matter, in other words, of straightening out the peck-order hierarchy among intracranial control agents. There exists within the cranium a whole world of diverse causal forces; what is more, there are forces within forces within forces, as in no other cubic half-foot of universe that we know. At the lowermost levels in this system, we have local aggregates of some sixty or more types of subnuclear particles interacting with great energy, all within the neutrons and protons of their respective atomic nuclei. These chaps, of course, do not have very much to say about what goes on in the affairs of the brain. We can pretty well forget them, because they are all firmly trapped and kept in line by their atomic overseers. The atomic nuclei and associated electrons are also, of course, firmly controlled in turn. The various atomic elements are "molecule-bound" — that is, they are hauled and pushed around by the larger spatial and configurational forces of their encompassing molecules.

Similarly, the molecules of the brain are themselves pretty well bound up and ordered around by their respective cells and tissues. Along with all of their internal atomic and subnuclear parts and their neighboring molecular partners, the brain molecules are obliged to submit to a course of activity in time and space that is very largely determined, for the lifetime of any given cell, by the over-all dynamic and spatial properties of the whole cell as an entity. Even the brain cells, however, with their long fibers and impulse-conducting properties, do not have very much to say about when they are going to fire their messages, for example, or in what time pattern they will fire them. The firing orders for the day come from a higher command.

In other words, the flow and the timing of impulse traffic through any brain cell, or even a nucleus of cells in the brain, are governed largely by the over-all encompassing properties of the whole cerebral circuit system, within which the given cells and fibers are incorporated, and also by the relationship of this circuit system to other circuit systems. Further, the dynamic properties of the cerebral system as a whole, and the way in which these properties direct and govern the flow of impulse traffic throughout the system — that is, the general circuit properties of the whole brain — may undergo radical and widespread changes from one moment to the next with just the flick of a cerebral facilitatory "set." This set is a shifting pattern of central excitation that will open or prime one group of circuit pathways with its own special pattern properties, while at the same time closing, repressing, or inhibiting endless other circuit potentialities that might otherwise be open and available for impulse traffic. These changes of "set" are responsible, for example, for such things as a shift of attention, a turn of thought, a change of feeling, or a new insight. To make a long story short, if one keeps climbing upward in the chain of command within the brain, one finds at the very top those over-all organizational forces and dynamic properties of the large patterns of cerebral excitation that are correlated with mental states or psychic activity. And this brings us close to the main issue.

We can take this argument a step further by looking at an illustrative example of one of these mental entities. For simplicity, let us consider an elemental sensation. Instead of philosophy's old favorite, the color red (the philosophic and geographic locus of which seems sometimes to be in some doubt), let us use another example, pain. To be more specific, let us say we are talking about pain in the fingers and thumb of the left hand, and let us pin it down further to pain in the left hand of an arm that was amputated above the elbow some months previously. You will recall that the suffering caused by pain localized mentally in a phantom limb is no easier to bear than that in a limb that is still there. It will be easier, however, by using this example, for us to infer where our conscious awareness does not reside.

In regard to the pain in a phantom limb, my contention is that any groans it may elicit from our patient and any other response measures or behavioral outputs that may be taken to be the result of the pain sensation are indeed caused not by the

80

biophysics, chemistry, or physiology of the cerebral nerve impulses as such, but by the pain quality, the pain property, per se. This brings us, then, to the real crux of the argument. Nerve excitations are just as common to pleasure, of course, as to pain, and the same is true of any other sensation. What is critical is that unique patterning of cerebral excitation that produces pain instead of something else. It is the over-all functional property of this pain pattern as a pattern that is critical in the causal sequence of brain affairs. This pattern has a dynamic entity, the qualitative effect of which must be conceived functionally and operationally and in terms of its impact on a living, unanesthesized cerebral system. It is this over-all pattern effect in brain dynamics that is the pain quality of inner experience. To try to explain the pain pattern or any other mental qualities only in terms of the spatiotemporal arrangement of nerve impulses, without reference to the mental properties and the mental qualities themselves, would be as formidable as trying to describe any of the endless variety of complex molecular reactions known to biochemistry wholly in terms of the properties of the electron, proton, and neutron and their subnuclear particles plus (and this, of course, is critical) their spatiotemporal relationships. By including the spatiotemporal relations, such a description becomes feasible in theory, probably, but fantastically impractical. Moreover, by the time science arrives at a point where it can describe the critical details of the impulse pattern of a mental experience in the functional terms and setting required, it will be describing, in effect, the conscious force or property itself. When we reach such a point, the conscious force will be recognized as such, and we shall be calling it just that — or at least that is the hypothesis I am putting forward.

Many readers will note my reliance throughout this discussion on the emergent concepts of T. H. Morgan and the corresponding configurational and field concepts of Gestalt psychology. The Gestalt schools of psychology and philosophy went wrong only when they moved into the brain and tried to transfer their pattern properties directly from the outside world and sensory surfaces into the cerebral cortex. The central, emergent conscious force within the brain, as visualized here, is not a simple surrounding envelope, or volume property, or any other kind of "isomorph," as the Gestalt schools tried to make it. It is rather a functional pattern that has to be worked out in entirely new terms, that is, in terms of the functional circuitry of the brain, in terms of the still unknown brain code.

Above simple pain and other sensations in brain dynamics, we find, of course, the more complex but equally potent forces of perception, emotion, reason, belief, insight, judgment, cognition, and all the rest. In the onward flow of conscious brain states, one state calling up the next, these are the kinds of dynamic entities that call the plays. It is exactly these encompassing mental forces that direct and govern the inner impulse traffic, including its electrochemical and biophysical aspects. When trying to visualize mental properties as they have been described, it is important to keep in mind the fact that all of the simpler, more primitive, electric, atomic, molecular, cellular, and physiological forces remain present, of course, and they all continue to operate. None has been cancelled; but these lower level forces and properties have been superseded, encompassed, as it were, by those forces of successively higher organizational entities. We must remember in particular that, for the transmission of nerve impulses, all of the usual electrical, chemical, and physiological laws still apply at the level of the cell, the fiber, and the synaptic junction. We must remember further that proper function in the uppermost levels always depends on normal operation at subsidiary levels.

Near the apex of this command system in the brain — to return to more humanistic concerns — we find ideas. Man over the chimpanzee has ideas and ideals. In the brain model proposed here, the causal potency of an idea, or an ideal, becomes just as real as that of a molecule, a cell, or a nerve impulse. Ideas cause ideas and help evolve new ideas. They interact with each other and with other mental forces in the same brain, in neighboring brains, and thanks to global communication, in far distant, foreign brains. And they also interact with the external surroundings to produce in toto a burstwise advance in evolution that is far beyond anything to hit the evolutionary scene yet, including the emergence of the living cell.

In the proposed scheme, the interplay of psychic and mental forces, though accessible — like the interior of the earth — only indirectly at this date becomes, in principle, a proper phenomenon for scientific investigation. Aside from problems of complexity and adequate technology, there would seem to be no great obstacle in principle to the eventual objective, scientific treatment of mental phenomena. One may see statements in the literature these days discouraging the hope that the mind is capable of explaining itself in terms of its own ideas; the argument is that no machine, living or otherwise, can logically embody within itself a complete description of itself. When you read such statements, however, always underline that word "complete" and then consider the extent of the explanatory possibilities that still remain even though they fall somewhat short of complete. Underline also that word "itself" and remember that this kind of logic does not prevent a man's mind from acquiring a complete description of his neighbor's mind or from passing on this description to other neighbors, excepting only the one he has described.

For an outside, second, brain, however, to directly experience the subjective qualities in an observed brain, it would seem to be necessary for the detector brain in the observer to be coupled in parallel to the emitting brain and wired directly into the specialized cerebral circuitry involved. This does not look very feasible under ordinary conditions for the near future. However, we do seem to be approaching exactly this situation experimentally in recent studies in which the brains of cats and monkeys have been bisected down the midplane into right and left halves. In the surgical process, we may leave a few cross-connections, coupling selected cerebral centers between "mind-right" and "mind-left." When the midline disconnection is complete, two separate mentalities are the result, which sense, perceive, learn, and remember independently. Each half seems to have its own realm of conscious awareness, and each is apparently as much out of contact with the inner experience of the other as are two brains in separate skulls. But when a band of cross-connections is left intact, linking, for example, the right and left centers for vision or those for touch sensibility in the hands, the inner, mental, subjective experience of the one brain seems to become available to the other.

Something of the kind can also be seen in studies of human patients who have had a similar surgical disconnection of the hemispheres for medical or therapeutic purposes and in whom cross-connections have been left intact between the lower brain centers involved in emotion and feeling. Whereas the cognitive, perceptual, mnemonic, and related experiences of mind-right in these people seem to be entirely out of touch with the corresponding experiences of mind-left, each brain half seems to share the emotional experience of the other. For example, if an emotion is triggered through vision by the introduction of an unexpected pin-up picture of a nude into a sequence of ordinary geometric pattern stimuli being projected into only one brain half, it is quite apparent from the verbal readout through the other half of the brain (that is, the one not directly excited) that this second hemisphere also feels properly embarrassed — or whatever the case may be. The second hemisphere, however, has no idea why it has these inner feelings and is unable to describe their source.

Looking back from this point, you will note that the earlier basic distinction or dichotomy between mentalism and materialism is resolved in this interpretation, and the former polar differences with respect to human values, when recast in the present scheme, become mainly errors of reductionism. This may be easily recognized as the old "nothing but" fallacy; that is, the tendency, in the present case, to reduce mind to nothing but brain mechanism, or thought to nothing but a flow of nerve impulses. For those acquainted with theories of mind, the new twist here, if any, is to be found in the attempt to make the emergent properties of inner experience conform to the inner brain code, rather than to the outside world or subjective impressions or sensory patterns; combined, of course, with the critical interjection of these mental qualities into the causal sequence. Note that we have not rejected the objective approach of science; it is an objective explanatory model that we are discussing. Our quarrel is not with the objective approach but with the long accepted demand for exclusion of mental forces, psychic properties, and conscious qualities — what the physicist might class as "higher-order effects" or "co-operative effects" — from the objective scientific explanation.

The present scheme would put mind back into the brain of objective science and in a position of top command. If correct, it would eliminate the old dualistic confusions, the dichotomies and the paradoxes, proposing instead a single unified system extending from subnuclear forces near the bottom up through ideas at the top. As a scientific theory of mind, it would provide a long sought unifying view on which to base our conception of human nature, the kind of view whose lack has recently been deplored in leading articles in *Science* and elsewhere. Moreover, this scheme suggests a possible answer not only for the relation between mind and brain but also for that between the outside world and its inner cerebral representation, another conundrum since the days of Plato. When used as a conceptual skeleton on which to build a body of philosophy, this theory tends to favor somewhat a single "this world" measuring stick for evaluating man and existence. As for the older materialist doctrine, one can say, in summary, that the denial or downgrading of conscious mental forces in objective experimental psychology during the past half-century has been tremendously valuable and successful as a tactical expedient for a developing science. It is hardly a doctrine, however, on which to build societal philosophy and cultural values.

Free Will

Let us shift gears at this point and consider another outcome of the mind-brain sciences that appears to run a close second in its threat to cherished images of human nature. This humanist "Enemy Number 2" to which I refer (some would rate it Number 1) is the scientific rejection of free will. Every advance in the science of behavior, whether it has come from the psychiatrist's couch, from microelectrode recording, or from the use of psychotropic drugs, brain splitting, Skinner boxes or the electron microscope, seems only to reinforce that old suspicion that free will is just an illusion. Like most others in brain research, I work on the assumption that every apparently free mental choice that I or anyone else has ever made must in fact have been causally predetermined in the preceding brain states and related events. This means that any decision in which any of us has ever engaged could not possibly have had any other outcome. It means none of us, hearing or reading these words, had any real chance to be doing anything else at this particular moment. It means that we are now and always have been imprisoned, as it were, in the inexorable onward march of causal determinism.

Attempts to restore free will to the human brain by recourse to various forms of indeterminacy — physical, logical, emergent, or otherwise — have failed so far as I can see to do more than introduce a bit of unpredictable caprice into our comportment that most of us would prefer to be without. Neither science nor philosophy seems able to refute the old admonition that "the moving finger writes; and, having writ, moves on." And piety, wit, and tears still seem impotent to change this situation. I do not feel overly comfortable about this kind of thinking any more than anyone else, but as yet I have not found any way out of it.

But before we start drawing gloomy humanist deductions from this apparent inevitability, concluding that moral responsibility is thereby removed or, on the other hand, simply rejecting science and determinism on emotional grounds, we should bear in mind a few additional points. In the present scheme, these points add up to the conclusion that if we really did have freedom of choice we might very likely prefer not to have; that is, we might well prefer to leave determinism in control, exactly as science postulates. It should be clear by now that in the brain model described here, man is provided in large measure with the mental forces and the mental ability to determine his own actions. This scheme thus allows a high degree of freedom from outside forces as well as mastery over the inner cellular, molecular, and atomic aspects of brain activity. Depending on the state of one's will power, the model also allows considerable freedom from lower-level natural impulses and even from occasional thoughts, beliefs, and the like, though not, of course, from the whole complex. In other words, the kind of brain visualized here does indeed give man plenty of free will, provided we think of free will as self-determination. To a very real and large extent, a person does determine with his own mind what he is going to do from among a large number of possibilities. This does not mean, however, that he is free from the forces of his own decision-making machinery. In particular, what this present model does not do is to free a person from the combined effects of his own thoughts, his own reasoning, his own feeling, his own beliefs, ideals, and hopes, nor does it free him from his inherited makeup or his lifetime memories. All these and more, including, yes, unconscious desires, exert in the brain their due causal influence upon any mental decision, and the combined resultant determines the inevitable but self-determined and highly special and highly personal outcome. We thus come back to the question, Do we really want free will, in the sense of gaining freedom from our own minds, from our own selves, and hence, from everything most precious that makes us us?

There is a bit more to the story of how one may "learn to stop worrying about freedom and come to love determinism," but it boils down to the old saying, "If you can't lick 'em, join 'em." Or as Confucius might have said, "If fate inevitable, relax and enjoy." Or to put it more directly, "There may be worse fates than causal determinism." Maybe after all it is better to be imbedded firmly in the causal flow of cosmic forces, as an integral part thereof, than to be on the loose and out of contact with these forces — free-floating as it were — with behavioral possibilities that have no antecedent cause and hence no reason or any reliability when it comes to future plans, predictions, or promises. I suspect, in fact, that if you were assigned the task of trying to design and build the perfect free-will model (let us say the perfect all-wise decision-making machine to top all competitors' decision-making machines), it is possible that you might decide that your aim should not be so much to free the machinery from causal contact as the opposite; that is, to try to incorporate into your model the potential value of universal causal contact — in other words, contact with all related information in proper proportion, past, present, and future.

In any case, it is clear that the human brain has come a long way in evolution in exactly this direction when you consider the amount and the kind of causal factors that this multidimensional, intracranial vortex draws into itself, scans, and brings to bear on the process of turning out one of its pre-ordained decisions. Potentially included, thanks to memory, are the events and collected wisdom of most of a human lifetime. We can also include, potentially, given a trip to the library, the accumulated knowledge of all recorded history. And we must add to all the foregoing, thanks to reason and logic, much of the future forecast and predictive value extractable for all this data. Maybe the total falls a bit short of universal causal contact, maybe it's not quite up to the kind of thing that evolution has going for it over on Galaxy Nine, and maybe, in spite of all, any decision that comes out is still predetermined. Nevertheless, it still represents a very long jump in the direction of freedom from the primeval slime mold, the Jurassic sand dollar, or even the latest 1965 model Orangutan.[1]

We may note in passing that on the debit side of the ledger there is little in our proposed model for consciousness to bolster one's hopes either for extrasensory perception or for post-mortem perception. Similarly, pre-partum perception in the embryo

---

[1] This paragraph and the preceding one are taken almost verbatim from an earlier article, *Problems Outstanding in the Evolution of Brain Function: James Arthur Lecture of the Evolution of the Human Brain* (New York: American Museum of Natural History, 1964).

may be presumed not to amount to much until after the requisite cerebral machinery for conscious awareness has begun to attain functional maturity in the later months of fetal life and in subsequent postnatal development.

Plasticity of Human Nature and Inheritance of Behavior Traits

Finally, in connection with development, I must mention briefly certain other advances in the brain-behavior sciences that have resulted in important revisions during the past two decades in our general conception of human nature. These advances have concerned the extent to which behavior traits can be inherited and the extent to which human nature is plastic and subject to shaping by experience and environment.

Through most of the first part of this century and up until about twenty years ago, the view prevailed that the brain gets its start in fetal life as an essentially equipotential network, functionally unstructured, a blank slate, as it were, which is then gradually channelized from early fetal movements onward by functional trial and error, practice, conditioning, learning, and experience. The objective, materialist movement in psychology, which was established first in Russia, largely under the influence of Pavlov, and which appeared soon afterward in this country, pioneered by Watson, under the name "behaviorism," has been identified almost as much with the promotion and idolatry of the conditioned response as it has with the demotion and vilification of consciousness. In this doctrine the mind, or psyche, was believed to develop gradually out of a life-long chain of successive conditioned-reflex associations, starting in the infant from a few elementary reactions, like love and hate, fear and anger. The whole idea of the genetic inheritance of behavior patterns was forcibly renounced, until the term "instinct" became highly discredited in professional circles, its defamation almost equalling that of consciousness. In those days, the embryonic growth of brain pathways was believed to be by nature non-selective and diffuse, and the establishment of precise fiber connections was held to be unimportant anyway for orderly function. The nerve connections, once laid down, were thought to be able to undergo radical and wholesale rearrangement by surgery, injury, and regeneration without disrupting orderly function. In the scientific thinking of those times, the brain was endowed with an almost mysteriously omnipotent plasticity and readaptation capacity. In general, science seemed to be telling us through the twenties and thirties and into the early forties that the human brain and human nature as well were extreme in their malleability. It seemed at that time a scientifically sound conclusion that it would be possible, by means of an appropriate program of training and environmental conditioning, to shape human nature, and hence society, within wide limits into a desired mold.

Much of the basic scientific thinking and evidence behind this view has since suffered a series of severe upsets, leading to a current stand that is almost diametrically opposed to the earlier doctrines. Instead of a loose, universal plasticity in brain hookups, we now see a basic built-in wiring diagram, characteristic of the species and functionally rather rigid. Instead of diffuse, non-selective growth of nerve connections in brain development, we now see a very precise and highly ordered patterning of brain fiber pathways and connections, all strictly preregulated by specific genetic effects and cytochemical affinities. Where there used to be an outright denunciation of the whole concept of "instinct," we now accept the idea that an entire evolutionary tree can be worked out on the basis of inherited behavior patterns, just as it can be worked out on the basis of morphological or serological traits. The conditioned response, along with other forms of learning, continues to be recognized, of course, as a highly powerful modeling influence, especially in man, but only within limits much narrower than previously supposed.

Within the specialized fields of scientific inquiry involved here, the pendulum of opinion continues at this date to swing in the direction of inheritance. How far it will go can only be guessed. It is still too soon for the implications to have fully permeated even the neighboring scientific disciplines. What implications these changes in the basic brain-behavior sciences may have, if any, for more distant problems in the social sciences will take much longer to evaluate. The latter, of course, will have to be worked out in their own right and at their own level. In any case, it would seem that the evidence available today says that we should renounce, along with other aspects of the behavior-ist, materialist approach discussed above, the old Pavlovian-Watsonian conditioned-reflex theory of the psyche, with its radi-cal environmentalism that used to tell us that literally 99 per cent of human nature and mind is a product of experience and training.

Our re-examination of the materialist doctrine in psychology could be extended much further into matters far removed from those in which brain researchers feel at all comfortable. Let me only remind my readers that the peck-order of causal entities does not stop within the individual brain but goes on up into higher levels involving society and culture, various subentities of which must be properly credited with many of man's most re-markable and fantastic achievements.

Reference to society brings, of course, the pressing reminder that any attempt to upgrade human nature through a more idealistic conception of mind is bound these days to be over-whelmingly counteracted by the cold laws of mathematics and the devastating downgrading effect of surplus numbers on the worth of the individual. We do not need the third law of psycho-dynamics to tell us that the optimum carrying capacity of our globe is perhaps already exceeded from the standpoint of qual-ity, dignity, meaning, and value for the human individual. When we look at the rising threat posed by the effects of human surplus and its by-products on the hard-won and painstaking achievements of eons of evolution, we are inclined to forget our little ideological skirmish with materialism, along with most of the human betterment efforts of our times, as just another losing battle in the face of mounting humanity — effort down the drain, until some higher force in our mental hierarchy than natural impulse can be brought to bear.

When it comes to the future outlook and an attempt to make

predictions regarding the future of man, behavioral science is hampered by a technical difficulty, in that once the prediction is published and man becomes acquainted with what he is supposed to do, he is in a position to take the prediction into account and is apt to be just perverse enough to do the reverse. Keeping this in mind, we can forecast that our generation and future generations need not really worry about surplus numbers, or who will outbreed whom, or any of the other problems we have touched on above, because these and related matters promise to be settled shortly in that final fatal flare of fission fireworks.

But to return to the central concern of this essay — the impact of creeping materialism in the brain-behavior sciences — we can say in summary that it is possible to see today an objective, explanatory model of brain function that neither contradicts nor degrades but rather affirms age-old humanist values, ideals, and meaning in human endeavor. The noble, free, or heroic, the exalted or sublime, qualities — or the opposite, for that is how meanings arise — that the humanist formerly thought he could see in man and his activities are present in our model, much as history and common experience have always shown. Finally, for those who like to receive a take-home lesson, that of the foregoing is simple for scientist and humanist alike: Never underestimate the power of an ideal.

RELATED ARTICLES BY THE AUTHOR

"Embryogenesis of Behavioral Nerve Nets," in *Organogenesis*, ed. R. L. DeHaan and H. Ursprung (New York: Holt, Rinehart, & Winston, Inc., 1965).

"The Great Cerebral Commissure," *Scientific American*, CCX (1964), 42–52.

"Chemoaffinity in the Orderly Growth of Nerve Fiber Patterns and Connections," *Proceedings of the National Academy of Science*, L (1963), 703–10.

"Physiological Plasticity and Brain Circuit Theory," in *Biological and Biochemical Bases of Behavior*, ed. H. F. Harlow and C. N. Woolsey (Madison: University of Wisconsin Press, 1958), 401–24.

"Neurology and the Mind-Brain Problem," *American Scientist*, XL (1952), 291–312.

5

THE IMPACT OF THE CONCEPT OF CULTURE ON THE CONCEPT OF MAN

by Clifford Geertz

I

Toward the end of his recent study of the ideas used by tribal peoples, *La Pensée Sauvage*, the French anthropologist, Lévi-Strauss, remarks that scientific explanation does not consist, as we have been led to imagine, in the reduction of the complex to the simple. Rather, it consists, he says, in a substitution of a complexity more intelligible for one which is less. So far as the study of man is concerned, one may go even farther, I think, and argue that explanation often consists of substituting complex pictures for simple ones while striving somehow to retain the persuasive clarity that went with the simple ones.

Elegance remains, I suppose, a general scientific ideal; but in the social sciences, it is very often in departures from that ideal that truly creative developments occur. Scientific advancement commonly consists in a progressive complication of what once seemed a beautifully simple set of notions but now seems an unbearably simplistic one. It is after this sort of disenchantment occurs that intelligibility, and thus explanatory power, comes to rest on the possibility of substituting the involved but comprehensible for the involved but incomprehensible to which Lévi-

CLIFFORD GEERTZ is professor of anthropology at the University of Chicago.

Strauss refers. Whitehead once offered to the natural sciences the maxim: "Seek simplicity and distrust it"; to the social sciences he might well have offered "Seek complexity and order it."

Certainly, the study of culture has developed as though this maxim were being followed. The rise of a scientific concept of culture amounted to, or at least was connected with, the overthrow of the view of human nature dominant in the Enlightenment — a view that, whatever else may be said for or against it, was both clear and simple — and its replacement by a view not only more complicated but enormously less clear. The attempt to clarify it, to reconstruct an intelligible account of what man is, has underlain scientific thinking about culture ever since. Having sought complexity and, on a scale grander than they ever imagined, found it, anthropologists became entangled in a tortuous effort to order it. And the end is not yet in sight.

The Enlightenment view of man was, of course, that he was wholly of a piece with nature and shared in the general uniformity of composition which natural science, under Bacon's urging and Newton's guidance, had discovered there. There is, in brief, a human nature as regularly organized, as thoroughly invariant, and as marvelously simple as Newton's universe. Perhaps some of its laws are different, but there *are* laws; perhaps some of its immutability is obscured by the trappings of local fashion, but it *is* immutable.

A quotation that Lovejoy (whose magisterial analysis I am following here) gives from an Enlightenment historian, Mascou, presents the position with the useful bluntness one often finds in a minor writer:

> The stage setting [in different times and places] is, indeed, altered, the actors change their garb and their appearance; but their inward motions arise from the same desires and passions of men, and produce their effects in the vicissitudes of kingdoms and peoples.[1]

---

[1] Arthur O. Lovejoy, *Essays in the History of Ideas* (New York: G. P. Putnam's Sons, Capricorn Books, 1960), p. 173. © 1948 by The Johns Hopkins Press.

Now, this view is hardly one to be despised; nor, despite my easy references a moment ago to "overthrow," can it be said to have disappeared from contemporary anthropological thought. The notion that men are men under whatever guise and against whatever backdrop has not been replaced by "other mores, other beasts."

Yet, cast as it was, the Enlightenment concept of the nature of human nature had some much less acceptable implications, the main one being that, to quote Lovejoy himself this time, "anything of which the intelligibility, verifiability, or actual affirmation is limited to men of a special age, race, temperament, tradition or condition is [in and of itself] without truth or value, or at all events without importance to a reasonable man." [2] The great, vast variety of differences among men, in beliefs and values, in customs and institutions, both over time and from place to place, is essentially without significance in defining his nature. It consists of mere accretions, distortions even, overlaying and obscuring what is truly human — the constant, the general, the universal — in man.

Thus, in a passage now notorious, Dr. Johnson saw Shakespeare's genius to lie in the fact that "his characters are not modified by the customs of particular places, unpractised by the rest of the world; by the peculiarities of studies or professions, which can operate upon but small numbers; or by the accidents of transient fashions or temporary opinions." [3] And Racine regarded the success of his plays on classical themes as proof that "the taste of Paris . . . conforms to that of Athens; my spectators have been moved by the same things which, in other times, brought tears to the eyes of the most cultivated classes of Greece." [4]

The trouble with this kind of view, aside from the fact that it sounds comic coming from someone as profoundly English as

---

[2] *Ibid.*, p. 80.
[3] "Preface to Shakespeare," *Johnson on Shakespeare* (London: Oxford University Press, 1931), pp. 11–12.
[4] From the Preface to *Iphigénie*.

Johnson or as French as Racine, is that the image of a constant human nature independent of time, place, and circumstance, of studies and professions, transient fashions and temporary opinions, may be an illusion, that what man is may be so entangled with where he is, who he is, and what he believes that it is inseparable from them. It is precisely the consideration of such a possibility that led to the rise of the concept of culture and the decline of the uniformitarian view of man. Whatever else modern anthropology asserts— and it seems to have asserted almost everything at one time or another — it is firm in the conviction that men unmodified by the customs of particular places do not in fact exist, have never existed, and most important, could not in the very nature of the case exist. There is, there can be, no backstage where we can go to catch a glimpse of Mascou's actors as "real persons" lounging about in street clothes, disengaged from their profession, displaying with artless candor their spontaneous desires and unprompted passions. They may change their roles, their styles of acting, even the dramas in which they play; but — as Shakespeare himself of course remarked — they are always performing.

This circumstance makes the drawing of a line between what is natural, universal, and constant in man and what is conventional, local, and variable extraordinarily difficult. In fact, it suggests that to draw such a line is to falsify the human situation, or at least to misrender it seriously.

Consider Balinese trance. The Balinese fall into extreme dissociated states in which they perform all sorts of spectacular activities — biting off the heads of living chickens, stabbing themselves with daggers, throwing themselves wildly about, speaking with tongues, performing miraculous feats of equilibration, mimicking sexual intercourse, eating feces, and so on — rather more easily and much more suddenly than most of us fall asleep. Trance states are a crucial part of every ceremony. In some, fifty or sixty people may fall, one after the other ("like a string of firecrackers going off," as one observer puts it), emerging anywhere from five minutes to several hours later, totally unaware of what they have been doing and convinced, despite the amnesia, that they have had the most extraordinary and deeply satisfying experience a man can have. What does one learn about human nature from this sort of thing and from the thousand similarly peculiar things anthropologists discover, investigate, and describe? That the Balinese are peculiar sorts of beings, South Sea Martians? That they are just the same as we at base, but with some peculiar, but really incidental, customs we do not happen to have gone in for? That they are innately gifted or even instinctively driven in certain directions rather than others? Or that human nature does not exist and men are pure and simply what their culture makes them?

It is among such interpretations as these, all unsatisfactory, that anthropology has attempted to find its way to a more viable concept of man, one in which culture, and the variability of culture, would be taken into account rather than written off as caprice and prejudice and yet, at the same time, one in which the governing principle of the field, "the basic unity of mankind," would not be turned into an empty phrase. To take the giant step away from the uniformitarian view of human nature is, so far as the study of man is concerned, to leave the Garden. To entertain the idea that the diversity of custom across time and over space is not a mere matter of garb and appearance, of stage settings and comedic masques, is to entertain also the idea that humanity is as various in its essence as it is in its expression. And with that reflection some well-fastened philosophical moorings are loosed and an uneasy drifting into perilous waters begins.

Perilous, because if one discards the notion that Man, with a capital "M," is to be looked for "behind," "under," or "beyond" his customs and replaces it with the notion that he, uncapitalized, is to be looked for "in" them, one is in some danger of losing sight of him altogether. Either he dissolves, without residue, into his time and place, a child and perfect captive of his age, or he becomes a conscripted soldier in a vast Tolstoian army, engulfed in one or another of the terrible historical determinisms with which we have been plagued from Hegel forward. We have had, and to some extent still have, both of these aberrations in the social sciences — one marching under the banner of cultural relativism, the other under that of cultural evolution. But we also have had, and more commonly, attempts to avoid them by seeking in culture patterns themselves the defining elements of a human existence which, although not constant in expression, are yet distinctive in character.

II

Attempts to locate man amid the body of his customs have taken several directions, adopted diverse tactics; but they have all, or virtually all, proceeded in terms of a single over-all intellectual strategy: what I will call, so as to have a stick to beat it with, the "stratigraphic" conception of the relations between biological, psychological, social, and cultural factors in human life. In this conception, man is a composite of "levels," each superimposed upon those beneath it and underpinning those above it. As one analyzes man, one peels off layer after layer, each such layer being complete and irreducible in itself, revealing another, quite different sort of layer underneath. Strip off the motley forms of culture and one finds the structural and functional regularities of social organization. Peel off these in turn and one finds the underlying psychological factors — "basic needs" or what-have-you — that support and make them possible. Peel off psychological factors and one is left with the biological foundations — anatomical, physiological, neurological — of the whole edifice of human life.

The attraction of this sort of conceptualization, aside from the fact that it guaranteed the established academic disciplines their independence and sovereignty, was that it seemed to make it possible to have one's cake and eat it. One did not have to assert that man's culture was all there was to him in order to claim that it was, nonetheless, an essential and irreducible, even a paramount ingredient in his nature. Cultural facts could be interpreted against the background of non-cultural facts without either dissolving them into that background or dissolving that background into them. Man was a hierarchically stratified animal, a sort of evolutionary deposit, in whose definition each level — organic, psychological, social, and cultural — had an assigned and incontestable place. To see what he really was, we had to superimpose findings from the various relevant sciences — anthropology, sociology, psychology, biology — upon one another like so many patterns in a *moiré*; and when that was done, the cardinal importance of the cultural level, the only one distinctive to man, would naturally appear, as would what it had to tell us, in its own right, about what he really was. For the eighteenth-century image of man as the naked reasoner that appeared when he took his cultural costumes off, the anthropology of the late nineteenth and early twentieth centuries substituted the image of man as the transfigured animal that appeared when he put them on.

At the level of concrete research and specific analysis, this grand strategy came down, first, to a hunt for universals in culture, for empirical uniformities that, in the face of the diversity of customs around the world and over time, could be found everywhere in about the same form, and, second, to an effort to relate such universals, once found, to the established constants of human biology, psychology, and social organization. If some customs could be ferreted out of the cluttered catalogue of world culture as common to all local variants of it, and if these could then be connected in a determinate manner with certain invariant points of reference on the subcultural levels, then at least some progress might be made toward specifying which cultural traits are essential to human existence and which merely adventitious, peripheral, or ornamental. In such a way, anthropology could determine cultural dimensions of a concept of man commensurate with the dimensions provided, in a similar way, by biology, psychology, or sociology.

In essence, this is not altogether a new idea. The notion of a *consensus gentium* (a consensus of all mankind) — the notion that there are some things that all men will be found to agree upon as right, real, just, or attractive and that these things are, therefore, in fact right, real, just, or attractive — was present in the Enlightenment and probably, has been present in some form or another in all ages and climes. It is one of those ideas that occur to almost anyone sooner or later. Its development in modern anthropology, however — beginning with Clark Wissler's elaboration in the nineteen-twenties of what he called "the universal cultural pattern," through Bronislaw Malinowski's presentation of a list of "universal institutional types" in the early forties, up to G. P. Murdock's elaboration of a set of "common-denominators of culture" during and since World War II — added something new. It added the notion that, to quote Clyde Kluckhohn, perhaps the most persuasive of the *consensus gentium* theorists, "some aspects of culture take their specific forms solely as a result of historical accidents; others are tailored by forces which can properly be designated as universal." [5] With this, man's cultural life is split in two: part of it is, like Mascou's actors' garb, independent of men's Newtonian "inward motions"; part is an emanation of those motions themselves. The question that then arises is, Can this halfway house between the eighteenth and twentieth centuries really stand?

Whether it can or not depends on whether the dualism between empirically universal aspects of culture rooted in subcultural realities and empirically variable aspects not so rooted can be established and sustained. And this, in turn, demands (1) that the universals proposed be substantial ones and not empty categories; (2) that they be specifically grounded in particular biological, psychological, or sociological processes, not just vaguely associated with "underlying realities"; and (3) that they can convincingly be defended as core elements in a definition of humanity in comparison with which the much more numerous cultural particularities are of clearly secondary importance. On all three of these counts it seems to me that the *consensus gentium* approach fails; rather than moving toward the essentials of the human situation, it moves away from it.

---

[5] A. L. Kroeber (ed.), *Anthropology Today* (Chicago: University of Chicago Press, 1953), p. 516.

The reason the first of these requirements — that the proposed universals be substantial ones and not empty or near empty categories — has not been met is that it cannot. There is a logical conflict between asserting that, say, "religion," "marriage," or "property" are empirical universals and giving them very much in the way of specific content, for to say that they are empirical universals is to say that they have the same content, and to say they have the same content is to fly in the face of the undeniable fact that they do not. If one defines religion generally and indeterminately — as man's most fundamental orientation to reality, for example — then one cannot at the same time assign to that orientation a highly circumstantial content, for clearly what composes the most fundamental orientation to reality among the transported Aztecs, lifting pulsing hearts torn live from the chests of human sacrifices toward the heavens, is not what comprises it among the stolid Zuni, dancing their great mass supplications to the benevolent gods of rain. The obsessive ritualism and unbuttoned polytheism of the Hindus expresses a rather different view of what the really real is really like from the uncompromising monotheism and austere legalism of Sunni Islam. Even if one does try to get down to less abstract levels and assert, as Kluckhohn did, that a concept of the afterlife is universal or, as Malinowski did, that a sense of Providence is universal, the same contradiction haunts one. To make the generalization about an afterlife stand up alike for the Confucians and the Calvinists, the Zen Buddhists and the Tibetan Buddhists, one has to define it in most general terms, indeed — so general, in fact, that whatever force it seems to have virtually evaporates. So, too, with any notion of a "sense of Providence," which can include under its wing both Navaho notions about the relations of gods to men and Trobriand ones. And as with religion, so with "marriage," "trade," and all the rest of what A. L. Kroeber aptly called "fake universals," down to so seemingly tangible a matter as "shelter." That everywhere people mate and produce children, have some sense of mine and thine, and protect themselves in one fashion or another from rain and sun are

101

neither false nor, from some points of view, unimportant; but they are hardly very much help in drawing a portrait of man that will be a true and honest likeness and not an untenanted "John Q. Public" sort of cartoon.

My point, which should be clear and I hope will become even clearer in a moment, is not that there are no generalizations that can be made about man as man, save that he is a most various animal, or that the study of culture has nothing to contribute toward the uncovering of such generalizations. My point is that such generalizations are not to be discovered through a Baconian search for cultural universals, a kind of public-opinion polling of the world's peoples in search of a *consensus gentium* that does not in fact exist, and, further, that the attempt to do so leads to precisely the sort of relativism the whole approach was expressly designed to avoid. "Zuñi culture prizes restraint," Kluckhohn writes; "Kwakiutl culture encourages exhibitionism on the part of the individual. These are contrasting values, but in adhering to them the Zuñi and Kwakiutl show their allegiance to a universal value; the prizing of the distinctive norms of one's culture." [6] This is sheer evasion, but it is only more apparent, not more evasive, than discussions of cultural universals in general. What, after all, does it avail us to say, with Herskovits, that "morality is a universal, and so is enjoyment of beauty, and some standard for truth," if we are forced in the very next sentence, as he is, to add that "the many forms these concepts take are but products of the particular historical experience of the societies that manifest them"? [7] Once one abandons uniformitarianism, even if, like the *consensus gentium* theorists, only partially and uncertainly, relativism is a genuine danger; but it can be warded off only by facing directly and fully the diversities of human culture, the Zuñi's restraint and the Kwakiutl's exhibitionism, and embracing them within the body of one's concept

---

[6] Clyde Kluckhohn, *Culture and Behavior* (New York: Free Press of Glencoe, a division of The Macmillan Co., 1962), p. 280.

[7] Melville J. Herskovits, *Cultural Anthropology* (New York: Alfred A. Knopf, Inc., 1955), p. 364.

of man, not by gliding past them with vague tautologies and forceless banalities.

Of course, the difficulty of stating cultural universals which are at the same time substantial also hinders fulfilment of the second requirement facing the *consensus gentium* approach, that of grounding such universals in particular biological, psychological, or sociological processes. But there is more to it than that: the "stratigraphic" conceptualization of the relationships between cultural and non-cultural factors hinders such a grounding even more effectively. Once culture, psyche, society, and organism have been converted into separate scientific "levels," complete and autonomous in themselves, it is very hard to bring them back together again.

The most common way of trying to do so is through the utilization of what are called "invariant points of reference." These points are to be found, to quote one of the most famous statements of this strategy — the "Toward a Common Language for the Areas of the Social Sciences" memorandum produced by Talcott Parsons, Kluckhohn, O. H. Taylor, and others in the early forties —

> in the nature of social systems, in the biological and psychological nature of the component individuals, in the external situations in which they live and act, in the necessity of coordination in social systems. In [culture] . . . these "foci" of structure are never ignored. They must in some way be "adapted to" or "taken account of."

Cultural universals are conceived to be crystallized responses to these unevadable realities, institutionalized ways of coming to terms with them.

Analysis consists, then, of matching assumed universals to postulated underlying necessities, attempting to show there is some goodness of fit between the two. On the social level, reference is made to such irrefragable facts as that all societies, in order to persist, must reproduce their membership or allocate goods and services, hence the universality of some form of family or some form of trade. On the psychological level, recourse is had to basic needs like personal growth — hence the ubiquity of educational institutions — or to panhuman problems, like the Oedipal predicament — hence the ubiquity of punishing gods and nurturant goddesses. Biologically, there is metabolism and health; culturally, dining customs and curing procedures. And so on. The tack is to look at underlying human requirements of some sort or other and then to try to show that those aspects of culture that are universal are, to use Kluckhohn's figure again, "tailored" by these requirements.

The problem here is, again, not so much whether in a general way this sort of congruence exists but whether it is more than a loose and indeterminate one. It is not difficult to relate some human institutions to what science (or common sense) tells us are requirements for human existence, but it is very much more difficult to state this relationship in an unequivocal form. Not only does almost any institution serve a multiplicity of social, psychological, and organic needs (so that to say that marriage is a mere reflex of the social need to reproduce, or that dining customs are a reflex of metabolic necessities, is to court parody), but there is no way to state in any precise and testable way the interlevel relationships that are conceived to hold. Despite first appearances, there is no serious attempt here to apply the concepts and theories of biology, psychology, or even sociology to the analysis of culture (and, of course, not even a suggestion of the reverse exchange) but merely a placing of supposed facts from the cultural and subcultural levels side by side so as to induce a vague sense that some kind of relationship between them — an obscure sort of "tailoring" — obtains. There is no theoretical integration here at all but a mere correlation, and that intuitive, of separate findings. With the levels approach, we can never, even by invoking "invariant points of reference," construct genuine functional interconnections between cultural and non-cultural factors, only more or less persuasive analogies, parallelisms, suggestions, and affinities.

However, even if I am wrong (as, admittedly, many anthropologists would hold) in claiming that the *consensus gentium* approach can produce neither substantial universals nor specific connections between cultural and non-cultural phenomena to explain them, the question still remains whether such universals should be taken as the central elements in the definition of man, whether a lowest common denominator view of humanity is what we want anyway. This is, of course, now a philosophical question, not as such a scientific one; but the notion that the essence of what it means to be human is most clearly revealed in those features of human culture that are universal rather than in those that are distinctive to this people or that is a prejudice we are not necessarily obliged to share. Is it in grasping such general facts — that man has everywhere some sort of "religion" — or in grasping the richness of this religious phenomenon or that — Balinese trance or Indian ritualism, Aztec human sacrifice or Zuni rain dancing — that we grasp him? Is the fact that "marriage" is universal (if it is) as penetrating a comment on what we are as the facts concerning Himalayan polyandry, or those fantastic Australian marriage rules, or the elaborate bride-price systems of Bantu Africa? The comment that Cromwell was the most typical Englishman of his time precisely in that he was the oddest may be relevant in this connection, too: it may be in the cultural particularities of people — in their oddities — that some of the most instructive revelations of what it is to be generically human are to be found; and the main contribution of the science of anthropology to the construction — or reconstruction — of a concept of man may then lie in showing us how to find them.

III

The major reason why anthropologists have shied away from cultural particularities when it came to a question of defining man and have taken refuge instead in bloodless universals is that, faced as they are with the enormous variation in human behavior, they are haunted by a fear of historicism, of becoming lost in a whirl of cultural relativism so convulsive as to deprive them of any fixed bearings at all. Nor has there not been some occasion for such a fear: Ruth Benedict's *Patterns of Culture*, probably the most popular book in anthropology ever published in this country, with its strange conclusion that anything one group of people is inclined toward doing is worthy of respect by another, is perhaps only the most outstanding example of the awkward positions one can get into by giving oneself over rather too completely to what Marc Bloch called "the thrill of learning singular things." Yet the fear is a bogy. The notion that unless a cultural phenomenon is empirically universal it cannot reflect anything about the nature of man is about as logical as the notion that because sickle-cell anemia is, fortunately, not universal it cannot tell us anything about human genetic processes. It is not whether phenomena are empirically common that is critical in science — else why should Becquerel have been so interested in the peculiar behavior of uranium? — but whether they can be made to reveal the enduring natural processes that underly them. Seeing heaven in a grain of sand is not a trick only poets can accomplish.

In short, we need to look for systematic relationships among diverse phenomena, not for substantive identities among similar ones. And to do that with any effectiveness, we need to replace the "stratigraphic" conception of the relations between the various aspects of human existence with a synthetic one; that is, one in which biological, psychological, sociological, and cultural factors can be treated as variables within unitary systems of analysis. The establishment of a common language in the social sciences is not a matter of mere co-ordination of terminologies or, worse yet, of coining artificial new ones; nor is it a matter of imposing a single set of categories upon the area as a whole. It is a matter of integrating different types of theories and concepts in such a way that one can formulate meaningful propositions embodying findings now sequestered in separate fields of study.

In attempting to launch such an integration from the anthropological side and to reach, thereby, an exacter image of man, I want to propose two ideas. The first of these is that culture is best seen not as complexes of concrete behavior patterns— customs, usages, traditions, habit clusters — as has, by and large, been the case up to now, but as a set of control mechanisms — plans, recipes, rules, instructions (what computer engineers call "programs")— for the governing of behavior. The second is that man is precisely the animal most desperately dependent upon such extragenetic, outside-the-skin control mechanisms, such cultural programs, for ordering his behavior.

Neither of these ideas is entirely new, but a number of recent developments, both within anthropology and in other sciences (cybernetics, information theory, neurology, molecular genetics) have made them susceptible of more precise statement as well as lending them a degree of empirical support they did not previously have. And out of such reformulations of the concept of culture and of the role of culture in human life comes, in turn, a definition of man stressing not so much the empirical commonalities in his behavior, from place to place and time to time, but rather the mechanisms by whose agency the breadth and indeterminateness of his inherent capacities are reduced to the narrowness and specificity of his actual accomplishments. One of the most significant facts about us may finally be that we all begin with the natural equipment to live a thousand kinds of life but end in the end having lived only one.

The "control mechanism" view of culture begins with the assumption that human thought is basically both social and public — that its natural habitat is the house yard, the market place, and the town square. Thinking consists not of "happenings in the head" (though happenings there and elsewhere are necessary for it to occur) but of a traffic in what have been called, by G. H. Mead and others, significant symbols — words for the most part but also gestures, drawings, musical sounds, mechanical devices like clocks, or natural objects like jewels — anything, in fact, that is disengaged from its mere actuality and used to impose meaning upon experience. From the point of view of any particular individual, such symbols are largely given. He finds them already current in the community when he is born, and they remain, with some additions, subtractions, and partial alterations he may or may not have had a hand in, in circulation there after he dies. While he lives he uses them, or some of them, sometimes deliberately and with care, most often spontaneously and with ease, but always with the same end in view: to put a construction upon the events through which he lives, to orient himself within "the ongoing course of experienced things," to adopt a vivid phrase of John Dewey's.

Man is so in need of such symbolic sources of illumination to find his bearings in the world because the non-symbolic sort that are constitutionally ingrained in his body cast so diffused a light. The behavior patterns of lower animals are, at least to a much greater extent, given to them with their physical structure; genetic sources of information order their actions within much narrower ranges of variation, the narrower and more thorough-going the lower the animal. For man, what are innately given are extremely general response capacities, which, although they make possible far greater plasticity, complexity, and on the scattered occasions when everything works as it should, effectiveness of behavior, leave it much less precisely regulated. This, then, is the second face of our argument: Undirected by culture patterns — organized systems of significant symbols — man's behavior would be virtually ungovernable, a mere chaos of pointless acts and exploding emotions, his experience virtually shapeless. Culture, the accumulated totality of such patterns, is not just an ornament of human existence but — the principal basis of its specificity — an essential condition for it.

Within anthropology some of the most telling evidence in support of such a position comes from recent advances in our understanding of what used to be called the descent of man: the emergence of *Homo sapiens* out of his general primate background. Of these advances three are of critical importance: (1) the discarding of a sequential view of the relations between the physical evolution and the cultural development of man in favor of an overlap or interactive view; (2) the discovery that the bulk of the biological changes that produced modern man out of his most immediate progenitors took place in the central nervous system and most especially in the brain; (3) the realization that man is, in physical terms, an incomplete, an unfinished, animal; that what sets him off most graphically from non-men is less his sheer ability to learn (great as that is) than how much and what particular sorts of things he *has* to learn before he is able to function at all. Let me take each of these points in turn.

The traditional view of the relations between the biological and the cultural advance of man was that the former, the biological, was for all intents and purposes completed before the latter, the cultural, began. That is to say, it was again stratigraphic: Man's physical being evolved, through the usual mechanisms of genetic variation and natural selection, up to the point where his anatomical structure had arrived at more or less the status at which we find it today; then cultural development got underway. At some particular stage in his phylogenetic history, a marginal genetic change of some sort rendered him capable of producing and carrying culture, and thenceforth his form of adaptive response to environmental pressures was almost exclusively cultural rather than genetic. As he spread over the globe he wore furs in cold climates and loin cloths (or nothing at all) in warm ones; he didn't alter his innate mode of response to environmental temperature. He made weapons to extend his inherited predatory powers and cooked foods to render a wider range of them digestible. Man became man, the story continues, when, having crossed some mental Rubicon, he became able to transmit "knowledge, belief, law, morals, custom" (to quote the items of Sir Edward Tylor's classical definition of culture) to his descendents and his neighbors through teaching and to acquire them from his ancestors and his neighbors through learning. After that magical moment, the advance of the hominids depended almost entirely on cultural accumulation, on the slow growth of conventional practices, rather than, as it had for ages past, on physical organic change.

The only trouble is that such a moment does not seem to have existed. By the most recent estimates the transition to the cultural mode of life took the genus *Homo* over a million years to accomplish; and stretched out in such a manner, it involved not one or a handful of marginal genetic changes but a long, complex, and closely ordered sequence of them.

In the current view, the evolution of *Homo sapiens* — modern man — out of his immediate pre-*sapiens* background got definitively underway nearly two million years ago with the appearance of the now famous Australopithecines — the so-called ape men of southern and eastern Africa — and culminated with the emergence of *sapiens* himself only some one to two hundred thousand years ago. Thus, as at least elemental forms of cultural, or if you wish protocultural, activity (simple toolmaking, hunting, and so on) seem to have been present among some of the Australopithecines, there was an overlap of, as I say, well over a million years between the beginning of culture and the appearance of man as we know him today. The precise dates — which are tentative and which further research may alter in one direction or another — are not critical; what is critical is that there was an overlap and that it was a very extended one. The final phases (final to date, at any rate) of the phylogenetic history of man took place in the same grand geological era — the so-called Ice Age — as the initial phases of his cultural history. Men have birthdays, but man does not.

What this means is that culture, rather than being added on, so to speak, to a finished or virtually finished animal, was ingredient, and centrally ingredient, in the production of that animal itself. The slow, steady, almost glacial growth of culture through the Ice Age altered the balance of selection pressures for the evolving *Homo* in such a way as to play a major directive role in his evolution. The perfection of tools, the adoption of organized hunting and gathering practices, the beginnings of true family organization, the discovery of fire, and most critically, though it is as yet extremely difficult to trace it out in any detail, the increasing reliance upon systems of significant symbols (language, art, myth, ritual) for orientation, communication, and self-control all created for man a new environment to which he was then obliged to adapt. As culture, step by infinitesimal step, accumulated and developed, a selective advantage was given to those individuals in the population most able to take advantage of it — the effective hunter, the persistent gatherer, the adept toolmaker, the resourceful leader — until what had been a small-brained, protohuman *Homo australopithecus* became the large-brained fully human *Homo sapiens.* Between the cultural pattern, the body, and the brain, a positive feedback system was created in which each shaped the progress of the other, a system in which the interaction among increasing tool use, the changing anatomy of the hand, and the expanding representation of the thumb on the cortex is only one of the more graphic examples. By submitting himself to governance by symbolically mediated programs for producing artifacts, organizing social life, or expressing emotions, man determined, if unwittingly, the culminating stages of his own biological destiny. Quite literally, though quite inadvertently, he created himself.

Though, as I mentioned, there were a number of important changes in the gross anatomy of genus *Homo* during this period of his crystallization — in skull shape, dentition, thumb size, and so on — by far the most important and dramatic were those that evidently took place in the central nervous system; for this was the period when the human brain, and most particularly the forebrain, ballooned into its present top-heavy proportions. The technical problems are complicated and controversial here; but the main point is that though the Australopithecines had a torso and arm configuration not drastically different from our own, and a pelvis and leg formation at least well launched toward our own, they had cranial capacities hardly larger than those of the living apes — that is to say, about a third to a half of our own. What sets true men off most distinctly from protomen is apparently not over-all bodily form but complexity of nervous organization. The overlap period of cultural and biological change seems to have consisted in an intense concentration on neural development and perhaps asso-

111

ciated refinements of various behaviors — of the hands, bipedal locomotion, and so on — for which the basic anatomical foundations — mobile shoulders and wrists, a broadened ilium, and so on — had already been securely laid. In itself, this is perhaps not altogether startling; but, combined with what I have already said, it suggests some conclusions about what sort of animal man is that are, I think, rather far not only from those of the eighteenth century but from those of the anthropology of only ten or fifteen years ago.

Most bluntly, it suggests that there is no such thing as a human nature independent of culture. Men without culture would not be the clever savages of Golding's *Lord of the Flies* thrown back upon the cruel wisdom of their animal instincts; nor would they be the nature's noblemen of Enlightenment primitivism or even, as classical anthropological theory would imply, intrinsically talented apes who had somehow failed to find themselves. They would be unworkable monstrosities with very few useful instincts, fewer recognizable sentiments, and no intellect: mental basket cases. As our central nervous system — and most particularly its crowning curse and glory, the neocortex — grew up in great part in interaction with culture, it is incapable of directing our behavior or organizing our experience without the guidance provided by systems of significant symbols. What happened to us in the Ice Age is that we were obliged to abandon the regularity and precision of detailed genetic control over our conduct for the flexibility and adaptability of a more generalized, though of course no less real, genetic control over it. To supply the additional information necessary to be able to act, we were forced, in turn, to rely more and more heavily on cultural sources — the accumulated fund of significant symbols. Such symbols are thus not mere expressions, instrumentalities, or correlates of our biological, psychological, and social existence; they are prerequisites of it. Without men, no culture, certainly; but equally, and more significantly, without culture, no men.

We are, in sum, incomplete or unfinished animals who complete or finish ourselves through culture — and not through culture in general but through highly particular forms of it: Dobuan and Javanese, Hopi and Italian, upper-class and lower-class, academic and commercial. Man's great capacity for learning, his plasticity, has often been remarked, but what is even more critical is his extreme dependence upon a certain sort of learning: the attainment of concepts, the apprehension and application of specific systems of symbolic meaning. Beavers build dams, birds build nests, bees locate food, baboons organize social groups, and mice mate on the basis of forms of learning that rest predominantly on the instructions encoded in their genes and evoked by appropriate patterns of external stimuli: physical keys inserted into organic locks. But men build dams or shelters, locate food, organize their social groups, or find sexual partners under the guidance of instructions encoded in flow charts and blueprints, hunting lore, moral systems, and aesthetic judgments: conceptual structures molding formless talents.

We live, as one writer has neatly put it, in an "information gap." Between what our body tells us and what we have to know in order to function, there is a vacuum we must fill ourselves, and we fill it with information (or misinformation) provided by our culture. The boundary between what is innately controlled and what is culturally controlled in human behavior is an ill-defined and wavering one. Some things are, for all intents and purposes, entirely controlled intrinsically: we need no more cultural guidance to learn how to breathe than a fish needs to learn how to swim. Others are almost certainly largely cultural: we do not attempt to explain on a genetic basis why some men put their trust in centralized planning and others in the free market, though it might be an amusing exercise. Almost all complex human behavior is, of course, the vector outcome of the two. Our capacity to speak is surely innate; our capacity to speak English is surely cultural. Smiling at pleasing stimuli and frowning at unpleasing ones are surely in some degree genetically determined (even apes screw up their faces at noxious odors); but sardonic smiling and burlesque frowning are equally surely predominantly cultural, as is perhaps demonstrated by the Balinese definition of a madman as someone who, like an American, smiles when there is nothing to laugh at. Between the basic ground plans for our life that our genes lay down — the capacity to speak or to smile — and the precise behavior we in fact execute — speaking English in a certain tone of voice, smiling enigmatically in a delicate social situation — lies a complex set of significant symbols under whose direction we transform the first into the second, the ground plans into the activity.

Our ideas, our values, our acts, even our emotions, are, like our nervous system itself, cultural products — products manufactured, indeed, out of tendencies, capacities, and dispositions with which we were born, but manufactured none the less. Chartres is made of stone and glass. But it is not just stone and glass; it is a cathedral, and not only a cathedral, but a particular cathedral built at a particular time by certain members of a particular society. To understand what it means, to perceive it for what it is, you need to know rather more than the generic properties of stone and glass and rather more than what is common to all cathedrals. You need to understand also — and, in my opinion, most critically — the specific concepts of the relations between God, man, and architecture that, having governed its creation, it consequently embodies. It is no different with men: they, too, every last one of them, are cultural artifacts.

IV

Whatever differences they may show, the approaches to the definition of human nature adopted by the Enlightenment and by classical anthropology have one thing in common: they are both basically typological. They endeavor to construct an image of man as a model, an archetype, a Platonic idea or an Aristotelian form, with respect to which actual men — you, me, Churchill, Hitler, and the Bornean headhunter — are but reflections, distortions, approximations. In the Enlightenment case, the elements of this essential type were to be uncovered by stripping the trappings of culture away from actual men and seeing what then was left — natural man. In classical anthropology, it was to be uncovered by factoring out the commonalities in culture and seeing what then appeared — consensual man. In either case, the result is the same as tends to emerge in all typological approaches to scientific problems generally: the differences among individuals and among groups of individuals are rendered secondary. Individuality comes to be seen as eccentricity, distinctiveness as accidental deviation from the only legitimate object of study for the true scientist: the underlying, unchanging, normative type. In such an approach, however elaborately formulated and resourcefully defended, living detail is drowned in dead stereotype: we are in quest of a metaphysical entity, Man with a capital "M," in the interests of which we sacrifice the empirical entity we in fact encounter, man with a small "m."

The sacrifice is, however, as unnecessary as it is unavailing. There is no opposition between general theoretical understanding and circumstantial understanding, between synoptic vision and a fine eye for detail. It is, in fact, by its power to draw general propositions out of particular phenomena that a scientific theory — indeed, science itself — is to be judged. If we want to discover what man amounts to, we can only find it in what men are: and what men are, above all other things, is various. It is in understanding that variousness — its range, its nature, its basis, and its implications — that we shall come to construct a concept of human nature that, more than a statistical shadow and less than a primitivist dream, has both substance and truth.

It is here, to come round finally to my title, that the concept of culture has its impact on the concept of man. When seen as a set of symbolic devices for controlling behavior, extrasomatic sources of information, culture provides the link between what men are intrinsically capable of becoming and what they actually, one by one, in fact become. Becoming human is becoming individual, and we become individual under the guidance of cultural patterns, historically created systems of meaning in terms of which we give form, order, point, and direction to our lives. And the cultural patterns involved are not general but specific — not just "marriage" but a particular set of notions about what men and women are like, how spouses should treat one another, or who should properly marry whom; not just "religion" but belief in the wheel of karma, the observance of a month of fasting, or the practice of cattle sacrifice. Man is to be defined neither by his innate capacities alone, as the Enlightenment sought to do, nor by his actual behaviors alone, as much of contemporary social science seeks to do, but rather by the link between them, by the way in which the first is transformed into the second, his generic potentialities focused into his specific performances. It is in man's *career*, in its characteristic course, that we can discern, however dimly, his nature, and though culture is but one element in determining that course, it is hardly the least important. As culture shaped us as a single species — and is no doubt still shaping us — so too it shapes us as separate individuals. This, neither an unchanging subcultural self nor an established cross-cultural consensus, is what we really have in common.

Oddly enough — though on second thought, perhaps not so oddly — many of our subjects seem to realize this more clearly than we anthropologists ourselves. In Java, for example, where I have done much of my work, the people quite flatly say, "To be human is to be Javanese." Small children, boors, simpletons, the insane, the flagrantly immoral, are said to be *ndurung djawa*, "not yet Javanese." A "normal" adult capable of acting in terms of the highly elaborate system of etiquette, possessed of the delicate aesthetic perceptions associated with music, dance, drama, and textile design, responsive to the subtle promptings of the divine residing in the stillnesses of each individual's inward-turning consciousness, is *sampun djawa*, "already Javanese," that is, already human. To be human is not just to breathe; it is to control one's breathing, by yogalike techniques, so as to hear in inhalation and exhalation the literal voice of God pronouncing His own name — *hu Allah.* It is not just to talk; it is to utter the appropriate words and phrases in the appropriate social situations in the appropriate tone of voice and with the appropriate evasive indirection. It is not just to eat; it is to prefer certain foods cooked in certain ways and to follow a rigid table etiquette in consuming them. It is not even just to feel but to feel certain quite distinctively Javanese (and essentially untranslatable) emotions — "patience," "detachment," "resignation," "respect."

To be human here is thus not to be Everyman; it is to be a particular kind of man, and of course men differ: "Other fields," the Javanese say, "other grasshoppers." Within the society, differences are recognized, too — the way a rice peasant becomes human and Javanese differs from the way a civil servant does. This is not a matter of tolerance and ethical relativism, for not all ways of being human are regarded as equally admirable by far; the way the local Chinese go about it is, for example, intensely dispraised. The point is that there are different ways; and to shift to the anthropologist's perspective now, it is in a systematic review and analysis of these — of the Plains Indian's bravura, the Hindu's obsessiveness, the Frenchman's rationalism, the Berber's anarchism, the American's optimism (to list a series of tags I should not like to have to defend as such) — that we will find out what it is, or can be, to be a man.

We must, in short, descend into detail, past the misleading tags, past the metaphysical types, past the empty similarities to grasp firmly the essential character of not only the various cultures but the various sorts of individuals within each culture if we wish to encounter humanity face to face. In this area, the road to the general, to the revelatory, simplicities of science lies through a concern with the particular, the circumstantial, the concrete, but a concern organized and directed in terms of the sort of theoretical analyses that I have touched upon — analyses of physical evolution, of the functioning of the nervous system, of social organization, of psychological process, of cultural patterning, and so on — and, most especially, in terms of the interplay among them. That is to say, the road lies, like any genuine quest, through a terrifying complexity.

"Leave him alone for a moment or two," Robert Lowell writes, not as one might suspect of the anthropologist but of that other eccentric inquirer into the nature of man, Nathaniel Hawthorne.

> Leave him alone for a moment or two,
> and you'll see him with his head
> bent down, brooding, brooding,
> eyes fixed on some chip,
> some stone, some common plant,
> the commonest thing,
> as if it were the clue.
> The disturbed eyes rise,
> furtive, foiled, dissatisfied
> from meditation on the true
> and insignificant.[8]

Bent over his own chips, stones, and common plants, the anthropologist broods, too, upon the true and insignificant, glimpsing in it, or so he thinks, fleetingly and insecurely, the disturbing, changeful image of himself.

---

[8] Reprinted from "Hawthorne," in *For the Union Dead*, by permission of Farrar, Straus, & Giroux, Inc., and Faber & Faber, Ltd., p. 39. Copyright © 1964 by Robert Lowell.

6

THE SENSE OF CRISIS

by James M. Redfield

I was first asked to contribute to this series a piece on "The Future of Man"; I of course refused. I am a historian, and if I know anything at all, I know about certain corners of the past, nothing about the future. But there is a related question that interests me, for not everyone asks, "What is the future of man?" Marcus Aurelius, for instance, writes:

> You can see for yourself what has gone before — so many shifts of power. So also you can see what will happen, for it will all be formed the same. It is impossible to break the rhythm of the past. So it is the same to look at human life across forty years as across ten thousand. What more could you see? [1]

If the future is to be the same as the present, it is without interest to us. Nor is it enough for the future to be various; it must also be meaningful. Augustine writes:

> We know not why God makes this bad man rich or that good man poor . . . why the judge's corruption or the falsehood of the witnesses should send the innocent away condemned . . . why the wicked man should live sound and the good man bedrid. . . . Such contrasts as these, who could collect or recount?
> And even if these absurd contrasts were constant . . .

JAMES M. REDFIELD is associate professor in the Committee on Social Thought at the University of Chicago.
[1] Marcus Aurelius *Meditations* vii.49. Unless otherwise noted, the translations included in this essay are my own.

this might be referred to God's just judgment . . . that those who were not to lose eternal bliss should for a while be exercised by temporal crosses. . . .

But now, seeing that not only are the good afflicted and the bad exalted (which seems injustice), but the good also often enjoy good and the wicked evil; this proves God's judgment more inscrutable and his ways more unsearchable. . . .

And when we come to that great judgment . . . there we shall not only see all things clearly, but acknowledge all the judgments of God, from first to last, to be firmly founded upon justice. And there we shall learn . . . also why God's judgments are generally incomprehensible to us, and how just his judgment is in that point also.[2]

For both these men the sense of the future depends upon the sense of the past. Marcus asserts the monotony of the future because he finds the past monotonous. For Augustine the past is unintelligible except in the light of the transhistorical, of divine revelation; the history of the Hebrews and Romans has meaning only when interpreted by scripture. So also he expects no meaning in future history except in the light of that final revelation which will conclude history.

Perhaps, then, a historian is an appropriate person to ask about the future. The historian is professionally committed to finding variety and meaning in the past; he expects similar variety and meaning in the future. Furthermore, the question of the future of man does not arise in all ages, and therefore the question has a historical character. It arises in our age, and it has arisen in others. We can perhaps ask: In what kind of world do men wonder about the future, and what are the various ways of wondering? As a historian, I would like to suggest an answer to these questions, not for our age, but for the Greeks. The period I am going to talk about, for all of us in the European tradition, is the classical age; as such it has been redescribed and reinterpreted in every period which followed it. So we can

<hr/>

[2] Augustine *City of God* xx. 2 (Everyman's Library edition: trans. John Healey; rev. and ed. R. V. G. Tasker). Used by permission of E. P. Dutton & Co., Inc., and J. M. Dent & Sons, Ltd.

ask: How does the classical age look from here? And the answer might tell us something about ourselves.

In these remarks I am going to lean heavily on three terms: society, nature, and history. By "society" I mean not simply the way men live together but also their sense that this way of living constitutes a pattern with a meaning. By "nature" I mean the given ground of our activity, external and internal: our environment, our animal needs and desires, and also our tendency to satisfy those needs and desires at the expense of the order of society. By "history" I mean not simply annals, the record of what happened, but the sense that the past has a definite pattern and direction, that it is coming to something in the future.

History, society, and nature are interdependent terms. They all meet, for instance, in our conception of the primitive. The primitive state may be defined as that state in which the social is not yet distinguished from the natural. The primitive itself is prehistoric, but from a conception of the primitive all conceptions of history begin.

The first account of a primitive people in Greek is Homer's account of the Cyclopes, who

> have no red-painted ships; there are no carpenters among them who could build boats well-fitted with benches, boats that could get them from city to city going about, as men cross the sea, one to another.[3]
> They trust in the immortal gods; they do not sow crops with their hands nor plow, but without sowing or tillage, all things grow, wheat, barley, and vines which bear the clustering grapes, and the rain of Zeus gives them increase. They hold no public meetings where plans are made; they have no *themis*, but they live in the crags of the high mountains in hollow caves, and each one makes *themis* for his own wife and children; they pay no attention to one another.[4]

The savagery of the Cyclopes has two aspects. They have no technology, and they have no social organization. They have

---

[3] *Odyssey* ix.125–29.
[4] *Odyssey* ix.107–15.

no agriculture or boats, but (more important) they pay no attention to public opinion and hold no public meetings; therefore they have no *themis*.

Themis, in Homer, is the principle of civilized life. It governs man's relations with the gods — prayer and libation are *themis* [5] — and it governs private relations within the family. It is *themis* that a woman should weep when her husband has died [6] and that a son should embrace his father when he returns; [7] and the sexual act is the *themis* of a man and a woman. [8] But first and foremost *themis* is a principle of politics; *themis* opens and closes the assemblies of man [9] and of the gods on Olympus. [10] *Themis* is related to the *agorē*, the public meeting, as principle is related to fact. [11] It is *themis* to contradict your king in a public meeting; [12] it is *themis* to try the troops with words before sending them to battle. [13] *Themis* is the principle of cultivated public action.

In Homer *themis* is primary, technology secondary. Odysseus tests the Cyclops by asking him for the entertainment which is the *themis* of strangers. [14] Odysseus does not assume that the Cyclopes are savages because they live in caves; he tests them against the standard of society. The Cyclopes, however, do not entertain their guests; they eat them. Lack of *themis*, not lack of technology, marks them as savages. *Themis* is the characteristic human good, and man is distinguished from the feral savage by his ability to live in a society.

Technique enables us to conquer nature; it is essential to the economic life, the life of the household. The Cyclopes have no technique because nature gives them all they need without effort. Man is not so well placed; he must remake the resources of nature with labor and skill and turn them to his good. Through the technical-economic life we secure for ourselves the natural goods: survival, abundance, luxury, and health.

---

[5] *Odyssey* iii.45.

[6] *Odyssey* xiv.130.

[7] *Odyssey* xi.451.

[8] *Iliad* ix.134; cf. ix.276.

[9] *Odyssey* ii.68–69.

[10] *Iliad* xx.4–9.

[11] *Iliad* xi.807.

[12] *Iliad* ix.33.

[13] *Iliad* ii.73.

[14] *Odyssey* ix.266–71.

The natural goods are the goods we share with the animals; the Cyclopes, because they know no other good, are a kind of speaking animal. Man *qua* man has other purposes. In society we *use* the resources secured us by economics and technology, and we use them to secure the characteristic human goods: honor and excellence, what Homer calls *timē* and *aretē*. To secure the human good we must have public meetings, for the human good cannot be secured by conflict with nature; it arises only in society, as men act on one another and as their action is admired by their peers.

Homer's world is a world of fiction, developed in a poetic tradition; it is not a world in which anyone ever lived. In the frame of fiction, Homer can ignore economics, man's contest with nature. Homer's heroes all have assured private incomes, and even his slaves and beggars do not worry much about the next meal. The Homeric world is a purely human world; the poems treat of men's relations with one another, as man establishes his superiority to man in games, in entertainment, in single combat, and in debate. *Themis* is the center of the Homeric world, and the arena of *themis* is what Hannah Arendt calls "the space of appearance," the public realm where men define themselves as individuals by exercising their capacity for "sharing words and deeds."

Furthermore the Homeric heroes, in their public lives, do not pursue their interest; they prove themselves, but they do not enrich themselves. The greatest host is the man who gives the most lavish gifts; the greatest speaker is not the man who gets his own way but the man whose wisdom is approved by the folk. Even the prizes won in battle are not real wealth; they are like the prizes in the games, *keimēlia*, objects not for use but for show, kept to be admired or to be given away.[15] Not property but honor is the aim of action. Odysseus' contest with Penelope's suitors is an exception, but even here the poet devotes most of his energy to establishing Odysseus' moral superiority to his enemies.

---

[15] Cf. M. I. Finley, *The World of Odysseus* (New York: Viking, 1954), pp. 58–59.

So trade, which is a public pursuit of self-interest, is nearly excluded from the Homeric poems. The heroes never trade, and the poet mentions trading only with derision, as the young Phaeacian derides Odysseus:

> You don't look, stranger, like a man skilled at games and all the business of men who are gathered. You look like a man used to going about in ships, a master of sailors and of men who sell things, concerned for his cargo, thinking always of the profit he's to make. You don't look like an athlete.[16]

The Homeric heroes are intensely competitive, but they compete like runners in a race, to excel one another; there is no place in the heroic pattern for the competition of the market place, for the man who buys low and sells high and enriches himself by impoverishing his neighbor. Competitive self-interest, the pursuit of the natural good, is a misuse of the public arena.

Because the Homeric frame of fiction excludes nature, it also excludes history. The social order is simply given, and as such it is unchangeable. The human order may be defined by contrast with the primitive life of the Cyclopes, but there is no notion that the human has emerged from the primitive. Man is man as unchangeably as god is god.

The Homeric world, in fact, transcends history. Because it is fictional, because it does not represent life in any period, it is valid in all periods. And throughout the history of the Greek nation the poems of Homer remained a model of the characteristically human world.

The oldest Greek poem describing a world of fact is probably Hesiod's *Works and Days,* roughly contemporary with the *Odyssey.* Hesiod describes the world as it happened to him, and for him economics is primary. For Hesiod trade is a necessary evil — certainly evil, but none the less necessary. Hesiod devotes one-tenth of his poem to a discussion of the best and worst seasons for trading; his judgment of the Spring selling season can stand for his judgment of trade in general:

---

[16] *Odyssey* viii.159–64.

124

I do not praise it. It brings no pleasure to my heart; it goes by too fast. It is hard to stay out of trouble, but all the same, men pursue it in the witlessness of their minds, for money is become the soul for us miserable mortals.[17]

Man, for Hesiod, is a greedy bargaining creature, always after his neighbor's goods. All of life, public and private, is the pursuit of interest; in the public arena we enrich ourselves at the expense of other people; in our private activity we gather wealth from nature. There are, he says, two kinds of strife. One, "evil war and quarreling," [18] is the strife of man against man; it is to be avoided. The other "Zeus has hidden . . . in the roots of the earth, and it is much better for man." [19]

Do not let malicious strife keep you from labor, a spectator at the quarrels of the meeting place. A man has little time for quarrels and meetings if he does not have an ample store laid up in his house, the harvest of the seasons that the earth brings forth.[20]

When Hesiod thinks of public activity he doesn't think of debate, the display of wisdom before the folk, but litigation, in which men lay claim to the property of others and frequently, by bribery and false witness, obtain it. The introduction of trade and the trader's values into the public world has destroyed the security of that world. The meeting of men together is not, as in Homer, a place for the *use* of private resources; rather it is a place where those resources are risked and often lost. There is only one security: to retire into a private world and labor to secure one's own possessions.

. . . Hated of gods and men is the man who lives without labor, like a drone among bees. . . . From labor men become rich in flocks and fat. . . . The lazy man envies the laborer, for labor makes wealth, and with wealth, honor. Whatever your fate, labor is best; turn a temperate heart

---

[17] *Works and Days* 682–86.
[18] *Works and Days* 14.
[19] *Works and Days* 18–19.
[20] *Works and Days* 28–32.

from the holdings of others, and tend your own life with labor. . . .

Wealth should not be taken; it is better as god's gift. When someone with the strength of his hands seizes riches or wheedles them with his tongue, as often happens when gain beguiles the mind of men and shamelessness treads down shame — easily the gods will wither him, wither his house; briefly his prosperity lasts . . . so keep your heart altogether from that. As best you can, make sacrifice to the gods. . . . Then will their angry mind to you be mild. You will buy another's land; he won't buy yours.[21]

Man must labor incessantly because nature is not fitted to his needs. "The earth is full of troubles, and the sea is full." [22] "The Gods keep hidden from men their livelihood; otherwise we would easily labor one day and keep ourselves for a year in idleness." [23] Man is alienated from nature, and the world in which we live is nearly the worst of possible worlds, a world of sickness, trouble, and swift old age. The task of the subsistence farmer is to create for himself an island of security between a hostile society and a hostile environment.

But these two are not really separate; the recalcitrance of nature is a reflection of the corruption of man.

For those who give straight judgment to stranger and citizen and do not transgress justice, their city flourishes; the folk there prosper. Peace, the nurse of youth, is on their land. . . . The earth gives them life in plenty; on the mountains their oaks bear acorns at the top, bees in the middle. Their thick-fleeced sheep bristle with wool; the women bear children like unto their parents; they flourish with goods continual, nor do they go about in ships, but the fertile soil bears fruit.

But where there is evil crime and shameless acts, Zeus marks them out for his justice; and often a whole city has perished on account of one evil man who goes astray and craftily works at harm. For them from heaven Zeus has

---

[21] *Works and Days* 303–41.

[22] *Works and Days* 101.

[23] *Works and Days* 42–45.

fixed great sorrow, famine and plague together. The people die, the women do not bear, and the households wither.[24]

In Hesiod, as in Homer, society is primary. Because Hesiod has lost confidence in society, he cannot approach nature with confidence. His society has isolated him and made him vulnerable to the recalcitrance of nature.

In Hesiod, as in Homer, the characteristic human good distinguishes man from the feral savage. "This is the law that Zeus has fixed for humanity: for the fish and the beasts and the winged birds, that they eat one another, since they have no justice; to humanity he gave justice, and it is far the best." [25]

Justice, *dikē*, plays the same role in Hesiod that the sense of order, *themis*, plays in Homer. Both are principles which govern the relations between man and man, both have divine sanction,[26] and both are inherent in man *qua* man. But *themis* is a principle of action, *dikē* a principle of restraint. *Themis* brings men together; *dikē* keeps them apart. *Dikē* keeps men from lying, cheating, and stealing; it keeps each man to his own.

Society, for Hesiod, is feral; the characteristic human excellence develops in the private world. And this alienation of man from society, as it expresses itself in a sense of alienation from nature, also expresses itself in a sense of alienation from history. *Dikē* cannot support itself against the pressure of nature without the support of society.

> Today there is still some good mixed with evil, but Zeus will destroy this race of mortals. . . . Father will no longer be equable with son, nor son with father, nor guest with host, nor friend with friend. . . . There will be no gratitude for a man who keeps his oath, nor for a just man, nor for a good, but they will rather honor the man who commits crimes and evil. There will be no *dikē* in their hands, no sense of respect. . . . Then to Olympus, leaving the broad earth, wrapping their fair bodies in white robes, Restraint and the Moral Sense will pass to the race of the

---

[24] *Works and Days* 225–44.
[25] *Works and Days* 276–80.
[26] Cf. *Odyssey* xix.109–14 and *Works and Days* 225–37.

immortals, leaving men. They will leave endless sorrows to mortal men; there will be no cure for evil.[27]

The world order bears against *dikē*; soon the characteristic human will be lost in the chaos of nature, and human life will become totally unlivable. Society is moving toward the primitive.

So we find our three terms in Hesiod: society, nature, and history. For him society is corrupt, nature is recalcitrant, and history is regressive — and this, I think, is a compact, if bleak, world view.

Hesiod's poem is the first statement of one enduring Greek world picture; the *Works and Days* is the foundation of a tradition developed through the sixth and fifth centuries B.C. by the oligarchic poets, particularly by Theognis and Pindar. I would like to explore this development, but that would be another essay. Here I wish to contrast the oligarch tradition with an alternative which began to develop in the sixth century. I call it the "reform tradition"; its oldest source is the poems of Solon.

Solon shares with Hesiod his diagnosis of society: competitive self-interest is the source of public disorder.

> The citizens themselves wish to destroy their city in their folly, drawn on by money. . . . They do not know how to stop when they have enough, nor how to put in order a life of calm and moderate plenty; they become rich led on by crime. They are unsparing of sacred property and of public; eagerly each man steals what he can get, and they take no care for the solemn altars of *dikē*.[28]

Solon, in fact, is more radical than Hesiod; for Solon the characteristic public activity is not litigation, by which one man steals another's farm, but civil conflict and tyranny, by which a man can steal a whole city.[29] Nor is it possible, as in Hesiod, to withdraw into your own household: "The public evil comes into every house; the doors of the courtyard no longer will keep it

---

[27] *Works and Days* 179–201.
[28] Solon 4.5–14 (J. M. Edmonds' numbering).
[29] Solon 10.

out; it jumps the high fences, and it finds you somehow, even if you hide in the farthest nook of the building." [30] But for Solon the corruption of society is no longer a personal but a political problem, and as such it has a political solution.

My heart tells me to teach the Athenians this: bad government brings the greatest harm to a city, but good government brings to the light all order and propriety and often puts fetters on the unjust. It makes the rough smooth, it limits excess, it baffles crime . . . it limits the raging of harsh strife, and by it all human things become proper and wise.[31]

Hesiod was a moralist, Solon a lawgiver. Solon did not simply protest and withdraw; he took his protest to the community and set about reform. In this, Solon is characteristic of his age; in the late archaic period the Greek cities began to take hold of their situation. They began to use the public order to restrain man's feral nature; and in so doing they began the reconstruction of public life.

Solon's reforms were in the interest of everyone; therefore they were in the special interest of no one. Solon says that he stood in "no man's land"; [32] he worked for no party, and all parties were disappointed by his work. "Each thought he could get great wealth. . . . Now they are angry with me, and they all look at me crossly, as if I were their enemy." [33] Solon did not try to stop the pursuit of interest; he tried to moderate it by balancing the opposing forces on the assumption that public excellence would arise from the balance of private vices. His aim was not to improve the character of his countrymen but to protect them from one another; he sought to construct a public order in which competitive self-interest would no longer be dangerous.

Solon's morality is much like Hesiod's. Solon, too, believed in the moral sense, the characteristically human. Solon, too, was proud of his own virtues. But he did not try to impose his virtues

---

[30] Solon 4.27–30.
[31] Solon 4.31–40.
[32] Solon 37.8.
[33] Solon 34.

on the city; rather they served him for an Archimedean point, enabling him to stand outside and to moderate the contention of less virtuous men.

> If another man had held the whip, as I did, a contriving man and avaricious, he would not have held back the folk. If I had liked to do what one party wanted, and then another, the city had been widowed of many men. But I mingled my strength together from every source and turned about among them like a wolf among many dogs.[34]

Solon could have been a tyrant, but he was not. He could have been the tool of special interest, but he was not. He stood outside the conflict, "throwing his shield over both contenders."[35]

The lawgiver must be good; otherwise his laws cannot be good. After that it is a technical problem. If the lawgiver has virtue and technical skill, if he is an expert political workman, he can produce a community where virtue is encouraged and vice discouraged. And this state is as much the product of one man's skill as a poem is the product of the skill of the poet.

In a sense, we could say that Solon, in his reconstruction of the public order, was attempting to realize the Homeric *themis*. But *themis* is a principle of spontaneous human behavior; Solon's *eunomia*, good government, is an artificial product. The state, to adapt Burkhardt's phrase, has become a work of art.

For the moralist, nature sets a limit to activity; men and communities cannot pursue excellence beyond the bounds which nature has set. For the technician, on the other hand, nature is a beginning, an occasion for activity; if nature were not inadequate to the needs of man, technique would never have come into existence. As Hippocrates says of his own art:

> In the beginning the art of medicine would not have been discovered (for there would have been no need for it) or even looked for, if the same regime and diet had suited the healthy and the sick. . . . As it was, necessity itself caused medicine to be looked for and discovered, in that

---

[34] Solon 36.20–27.　　　[35] Solon 5.

when the sick used the same diet as the healthy it did them
no good, any more than it does now.[36]

Technique arises from need; its task is to fit nature to the needs
of man. Technique works by a process of trial and error, testing
the various resources of nature against the needs of man. By
refinement and selection, technique gradually creates an environment satisfactory to man. Hippocrates again:

> Those who discovered medicine . . . first diminished
> the quantity of food . . . and to some of the sick this was
> evidently a great help but not to all; there were some un-
> able to digest even a small amount of grain. Such patients
> evidently required something weaker; so the doctors dis-
> covered gruel, mixing a small quantity of strong food with
> a great amount of water and moderating the strength of
> the food by mixing and cooking it. And in some cases the
> patient could not digest the gruel; so the doctors went on
> and prescribed a liquid diet . . . taking care [in each
> case] not to prescribe anything stronger or weaker than
> what was required.[37]

In a sense technique moves away from nature; technique
transforms the natural environment. But in another sense technique moves toward nature; every step of the process is tested
against a standard of nature. The aim of technique is to produce
a kind of second nature by fitting out man with the skills and
habits he needs to live comfortably in his environment. The
invention of the technique, the remaking of human life, is full
of effort, but if the technique is successful, human life, to the
degree of its success, is effortless. As Democritus says: "Nature
and teaching are similar, for teaching transforms men, and as it
transforms them, it creates nature."[38] And Euenus: "The practice, my friend, takes a long time, but then as it comes to com-
pletion, it is nature."[39]

---

[36] *Ancient Medicine* 3.
[37] *Ancient Medicine* 5.
[38] Democritus B33 (Herman Diels's numbering).
[39] Euenus 9 (J. M. Edmonds' numbering).

So, as man moves from the primitive to the cultivated, he does not simply struggle with the difficulties of his world; he actually creates a new world for himself. To this creation we give the name of progress. Hippocrates sees it very clearly; for him progress does not exist merely in the specialized arts but in the general habits of practice characteristic of cultivated life.

To start from the earliest times: I don't think the diet now in use among the healthy would have been discovered if it had suited men to eat what oxen and horses eat . . . raw grain and twigs and grass. The animals flourish on such food and have no need of any other diet, and in the beginning, I imagine men too made use of such a diet. Our present diet, I imagine, was discovered and worked out over a long period of time, since men suffered greatly from this animal . . . diet . . . just as we would now suffer from it. . . . Perhaps they suffered less, as they were used to it, but they suffered all the same, so that the majority and those with the weakest natures died, most likely, while the strongest held out a little longer. . . . Because of this suffering, I imagine, men sought some diet fitting to their nature and found it; I mean the diet we now use. They took the grain, soaked it, husked it, ground it, sifted it, mixed it, and made bread . . . fitting it to the nature and capacity of man.[40]

Here again society and nature echo one another; as men began to reform the state they become confident of their ability to master nature. The late archaic period was a time of hope; men were proud of what they had accomplished, and they expected to accomplish more. Hippocrates again: "There is a path of discovery; by it we have discovered all that we have discovered over this expanse of time. And the rest can be discovered, too . . . if only, starting from what we already know, we go on and look for it."[41]

Earlier I said that Solon's state was an artificial product. But his state was not really an artifact; rather it was an invention—

---

[40] *Ancient Medicine* 3.   [41] *Ancient Medicine* 2.

not a thing but a way of doing things. Its creation was analogous, not to making a pot, but to inventing the potter's wheel. Like any inventor, Solon intended his way of doing things to be a permanent addition to the cultivated life of man. And like any invention, Solon's state was subject to improvement, as it was tested and retested against the ground of nature. Solon's reforms were completed by about 580 B.C., but the next one hundred fifty years of Athenian history were in the hands of a sequence of political innovators, each building on his predecessor's work: Solon, Peisistratus, Cleisthenes, Themistocles, Ephialtes, and Pericles. In Pericles' funeral oration Thucydides gives us a description of the state which was the culmination of this process. The Athenians, says Pericles, have conquered material nature; the mark of this conquest is their high standard of living and their leisure.

> Our public order procures us the greatest rest from labor; we have institutionalized games and annual festivals, along with fine private celebrations, whose daily delight drives out sorrow. And because of the strength of our city, there come here the products of all the earth, so that, as a consequence, we expect to enjoy other people's produce just as certainly as our own.[42]

More important, Athens has conquered man's animal nature by providing a moderated arena for the competitive pursuit of self-interest; Athens has assimilated into its social order the commercial economy.

> Wealth we value rather for the occasions of its use than for boasting about it, and no one thinks poverty shameful but rather not to attempt to escape it. Furthermore, economic activity and political activity belong to the same people. . . . We are the only city which holds a man who takes not part in politics to be not a decent sort but rather useless.[43]

---

[42] Thucydides *History of the Peloponnesian War* ii.38 [hereinafter referred to as Thucydides].

[43] Thucydides ii.40.1–2.

For the oligarchic tradition, human excellence lay in withdrawal from the competitive life of the public arena. Athenian political reform, on the other hand, *developed* the public arena so that *all* human activity could become a part of public excellence. Athens did succeed, in its own way, in reconstructing the Homeric *themis;* the standard of the community, as in Homer, became a standard, not of restraint, but of action. Athens was an open society; around a *laissez faire* economy it created a *laissez faire* society.

> Our political life is conducted on a basis of liberty, and in our day-to-day relations with one another, we are not suspicious of the behavior of our neighbor, nor are we angry with him if he lives in a way which suits himself, nor do we show toward him the kind of annoyance which, while it does no actual harm, is unpleasant for the man who observes it.[44]

Furthermore, Athens is a developed society, and her citizens have acquired the second-nature characteristic of such societies. The Athenians have developed a new sort of personal excellence, no longer laborious and habitual, but easy and intellectual.

> Some people [by which Pericles means the Spartans] make education a matter of laborious practice from earliest childhood and so get some share of courage; we live at ease and nonetheless when we approach danger are equal to it.[45]
> After all, if we are willing to run risks in an easy frame of mind and not because of laborious training, not because of our conditioning but out of the courageousness of our character, we get the added advantage of not having to suffer for difficulties which are yet to come; whereas when it does come to the point, we show ourselves as bold as those who are always working at it.[46]
> We do not think debate an obstacle to action; rather we think we ought to have fully explained to us what we are going to do. So here is another way in which we are exceptional; we are both able to be daring and to think through

---

[44] Thucydides ii.37.2.   [46] Thucydides ii.39.4.
[45] Thucydides ii.39.1.

what we are going to attempt. In other people ignorance produces boldness, systematic thought, hesitation. But surely one would be right to say that those have most developed their souls who have come to a clear understanding of what is fearful and what desirable and for that very reason do not shrink from danger.[47]

By her conquest of nature, Athens has built a human world. Athens is a comfortable, interesting, creative place; in Hippocrates' phrase, it is a society "fitted to the nature and capacities of man."

Athens is a pioneering, progressive society. In conquering nature and in remaking society, Athens is constructing her own history.

> To sum it all up, I would say that our whole city has become an education for Greece.[48]
> . . . We did not develop our public order in imitation of our neighbors' ways; rather we ourselves have become a pattern for others.[49]

Or as the Corinthians tell the Spartans in Book I:

> Your way of life is rather old-fashioned in comparison with theirs. And of necessity, just as in the case of technology, the new developments always make obsolete the old. . . . When people are compelled to do many things, they produce a stream of technical innovations; that is why the Athenians . . . far excel you in modernity.[50]

To sum up: for Pericles society is open, nature is malleable, and history is progressive. And in those three points I would sum up the world view of what we call the golden age.

A golden age is a fragile historical experience. It never lasts very long and it never includes a whole society; always it is something felt for a while by a few people. Given the fallen nature of man, such a synthesis can never be complete; always

---

[47] Thucydides ii.40.2–3.   [49] Thucydides ii.37.1.
[48] Thucydides ii.41.1.   [50] Thucydides i.71.3.

it contains the sources of its own dissolution. This is true of the Periclean synthesis as well.

Some ten years before the funeral oration Sophocles saw this and put it in the great ode of the *Antigone*:

Wonders are many, and none so wonderful as human-kind. It walks across the stormy back of the grey sea, faring where wave swallows wave; the oldest of the gods, the slackless, tireless earth, it has turned to its use, twisting the furrows year by year as the mules turn.

The tribe of frivolous birds he hunts, and the nation of ranging beasts, and the sea-spawn of the deep with net-spun coils, man the inventful. He prevails with his craft in the wild over hill-treading creatures, so that the thick-maned horse he brings under his double yoke, and the tireless hill-bred ox.

Speech, and thought like wind, and a spirit bred to the habit of towns he has taught himself, to escape from the misty hostile frost and the darts of rain; ever resourceful is he. Resourceless he comes to nothing before him; from death alone he has found no escape, but against the most difficult sickness he has contrived a release.

This clever contriver, holding to skill beyond hope, sometimes moves to evil, sometimes to good, walking in the laws of his country and keeping his oath in justice — high-citied he. But cityless he who is glad to dare what is shameful. May he never share my hearth or join me in council, the man who would do such things.[51]

Man has conquered nature, but he has not conquered him-self, and all his technical inventiveness will not enable him to do so. Technique, because it arises from the needs of nature, con only provide us with the natural goods: survival, abun-dance, health, and luxury. Morality, the characteristically human good, remains beyond the reach of skill. That is why we are always surest of the reality of progress when we think of agri-culture and medicine; that is why Hippocrates is the most optimistic of Greek writers. Medicine, in pursuing health, pur-sues a positive good, not the highest of human goods, but a

---

[51] Sophocles *Antigone* 332–75.

good none the less. The products of most technique are amoral, good or evil according to their use. As Socrates says in the *Gorgias*: the helmsman is a gifted man; he can take you to Egypt all right — but he doesn't know if it's a good thing for you to go there. And you wouldn't want him to marry your daughter.[52] Human excellence cannot be defined in relation to the conquest of nature but only in relation to the human good.

And that is why, however much of an artifact the state becomes, it still requires the Archimedean point, the moral sense of its maker. Pericles held such a position in the Athens he ruled; Thucydides says of him:

> He held his power by the excellence of his reputation and his judgment; it was obvious that he could not be bribed, and so he ruled the city like a free man . . . since he had not got his power by unworthy means. . . . It was called a democracy but was in fact the rule of one man. But those who came after him were more on a par with one another, and as each of them strove to be first, they . . . lost their hold on affairs.[53]

Even Pericles was not a moralist in the archaic sense. The funeral oration contains no mention of justice, or of god; Pericles praises the state for its success and for its size. But for him success and size are valuable, not in themselves, but because they are honorable: "Honor alone is ageless, and when you are worn with years it is not making money, as some say, that brings the greatest satisfaction, but being honored."[54] The Periclean state, like the Homeric, mastered nature in order to make possible the human good, the "sharing of words and deeds." Honor may have its roots in material success, but like justice, it is a transcendent principle. Pericles spoke as a man who stands above his society and contemplates it; no statesman after him achieved his Olympian perspective. The death of Pericles left the state of which he was the last inventor to run without the guidance of its maker, and this loss had moral consequences.

---

[52] Plato *Gorgias* 511c–512c.
[53] Thucydides ii.65.8–10.
[54] Thucydides ii.44.4.

One hundred fifty years of political innovation had accustomed the Athenians to the notion that the state and its rules are artifice. It is a short step to the notion that morality as a whole is artifice. The notion that morality is a human product was central to the Sophists; we find it, for example, set out by Plato's Protagoras.

Protagoras in Plato's dialogue tells a fable of the history of man. Man was ill-equipped by nature; so Prometheus provided him with technique. "At this early time," Protagoras says,

> men lived scattered without cities; so they were destroyed by the wild beasts since they were each of them too weak. The skills of the craftsmen were sufficient for their nourishment, but they were incapable of making war on the beasts, for they lacked the technique of politics, one part of which is the technique of war. So they tried to band together and save themselves by founding cities. When they were banded together, however, they wronged one another in that they did not possess the technique of politics; so again they were scattered and destroyed. So Zeus was afraid that our race would perish, and he sent Hermes to bring to men the sense of restraint and *dikē*, so that their cities could be ordered and they could be joined by bonds of friendship. . . . "Let them all partake of it," said Zeus, "for a city cannot exist if only some partake of *dikē*. . . . And set it down as my law that a man unable to partake of the sense of restraint and of *dikē* is to be killed as a menace to the body politic." [55]

Protagoras' fable is a naturalistic explanation of morality. Morality, he says, like technique, arises from the needs of nature; without morality man cannot organize himself against a hostile world. Morality, like technique, is a means to the natural good; morality is good because it enables man to survive.

Protagoras' fable appears to be a defense of *dikē*; in fact, the fable is an attack on it. By giving the human good a ground in nature, Protagoras makes man a part of nature; he dehumanizes humanity by denying the human good its special status. Once

---

[55] Plato *Protagoras* 322a-d.

morality is justified by an explanation of its origin and use, it becomes a means like any other and, as such, subject to criticism.

This criticism is immediate, for justice, as Protagoras describes it, is a good thing for men in general but not good for men in particular. The moral law enables a community to survive, but in the process each member of the community is restricted in his own pursuit of his own interest. So Protagoras' fable is restated by Callicles in the *Gorgias*, as a criticism of morality.

> I suppose that those who created laws were the weaker men and the multitude. Concerned for themselves and for their own advantage, they passed these laws; that is why they praise what they praise and blame what they blame. They were afraid of the stronger sort of men, the men who could take advantage of them; in order not to be taken advantage of, they say that taking advantage is disgraceful and wrong. . . . I suppose the weaker sort are pleased if they can even have an equal share, worthless though they are.[56]

And again by Glaucon in the *Republic*:

> Some people say that doing wrong is good and being wronged is bad but that being wronged exceeds in evil the goodness of doing wrong, so that once people had wronged one another and been wronged and had a taste of both, since they couldn't have one without the other, it seemed better to them to make a contract with one another neither to do nor suffer wrong. That was the beginning of our laws and contracts . . . and this is the origin and essence of justice, which is between the best thing, that one should do wrong without being punished, and the worst thing, that one should be wronged without the power of revenge.[57]

In my pursuit of the natural good, *other people's* justice is useful to me, as my justice is useful to them but not to myself. I would be best placed if I could treat other people badly while

---

[56] Plato *Gorgias* 483b-c. [57] Plato *Republic* 358e–359a.

they continued to treat me well. Of course, I would have to be careful: the community has sanctions against injustice, and I would have to avoid getting caught. And also, I, like any citizen, am dependent upon the stability of the community, and I would not want any injustice to threaten the community as a whole; I want to steal from other people's houses, but I don't want the police to become so demoralized that they stop protecting *my* property. But these are merely technical problems, difficult, perhaps, but not insoluble. Perhaps I could become such a clever talker that I could talk my way out of any kind of trouble. Perhaps I could become a tyrant and turn to my own use the whole apparatus of the state. I could be such a man as Glaucon describes:

> [A man] like the skilled steersman or doctor, able to distinguish what is within the range of his technique from what is not, and attempting only the former. Then, if he should get into difficulties, able to recover himself — and then going unnoticed. . . . For the man who is caught . . . is a poor sort; the most radical injustice is to seem to be just without being so. . . . Then, able to speak and persuade people, if someone informs on his injustice, and to use force where force is required, equipped with courage and strength, with well-organized friends and with money.[58]

Primitive man pursued his own interest and was incapable of living in a community. Later men learned to set aside their own interest and live in the interest of the community. But the most sophisticated man could successfully pursue his own interest within the community. The doctrine of the natural origin of morality thus became a program for the political radicals of the post-Periclean state. The Sophist Antiphon set it out:

> A man would employ that form of justice most beneficial to himself if he would treat the laws of great importance when he is in front of witnesses. When he is

---

[58] Plato *Republic* 360e–361b.

without witnesses, he should pay attention to nature. The laws have been constructed, but nature is by necessity. The standards of the law are not by nature but by agreement. . . . If a man transgress the law without being seen by those who agreed to it, he is not subject to shame or punishment; if they do notice him, he is. But if someone violates the order of nature, it doesn't matter if no one notices him; he suffers no less — it doesn't matter if everyone sees him; the suffering is no greater. For he is not injured by opinion but in truth.[59]

Antiphon denies the reality of that second nature which is a product of history. For him there is only one ground of nature; from it all action originates and toward its needs all action tends. Everything between is illusion.

In Pericles' notion of the state, man's animal nature was to be turned to the ends of society. For Callicles and Antiphon, society was to be turned to the ends of man's animal nature. The radicals celebrated the animal ground of humanity, the wild beast hidden in the civilized clothes. As Callicles says:

According to what sort of justice did Xerxes invade Greece or his father Scythia? . . . I think that in accordance with the justice of nature they did these things and, yes, by Zeus, according to the law of nature, but not perhaps the kind of law we enact. We shape the best and strongest among us, getting hold of them in childhood, as one might a lion cub; we charm and bewitch them and make them our slaves, saying that men should share equally and that this is justice and nobility. But if, I think, a man should grow up with a nature great enough, he would shake off all these things and break through them and make his escape, treading under foot our regulations and juggleries and charms and laws and all our restrictions on nature; then he would stand up and show himself, a master who has been our slave, and then would shine forth the justice that is nature's.[60]

---

[59] Antiphon Sophistes 4.10–53 (Louis Gernet's numbering).
[60] Plato Gorgias 483e–484a.

In a sense the difference between this position and the Periclean position is a small one; it is the difference between saying "society is artifice" and saying "society is mere artifice." For Pericles, man is an aggressive animal whose aggression can be shaped by a society so that it leaves to history a monument of honorable action. For Callicles and Antiphon, man is an aggressive animal pure and simple; back of all the complexities of society, he remains an animal still. The greatest men understand this and pursue their own interest without restraint or shame; they recover for themselves the primitive state. So when Euripides in the late fifth century wrote his play about the Cyclops he made his monster talk the language of the Athenian political radicals:

> Wealth, you human weakling, is the wise man's god;
> everything else is . . . fancy shapes of words. . . . I do
> not know that Zeus exists, a stronger god than I am; the
> rest does not concern me. . . . The earth by its necessity,
> whether it likes or not, brings forth the grass to feed my
> sheep. I sacrifice to no one but myself . . . and to the
> greatest god of all, my gut. To drink and eat, day after day,
> that is Zeus for men of sense, and not to hurt themselves.
> As for those who made up laws to complicate the lives of
> men — to hell with them. I'll not restrain myself from doing
> good to my own soul — by eating you.[61]

This is the ultimate statement of the pursuit of the natural good; here the story comes full circle. At the end of the long history of Greek social progress, we are back among the cannibals.

To sum up the radical position: society is weak illusion, nature is harsh reality, and history is meaningless. The appearance of this position upon the stage of society produced the Greek sense of crisis.

The sense of crisis did not arise among the radicals; Callicles and Antiphon were confident of victory in the war of all against all. The sense of crisis arose among men like Sophocles, Aristoph-

---

[61] Euripides *Cyclops* 316–41.

anes, and Plato, men concerned for the future of the human good in a world dominated by the radicals.

The radical position was so simple as to seem irrefutable. If society is artificial, it is technical. If it is technical, it is a tool for the use of those who understand it. If it is a tool, it is amoral — good if it is used well, evil if it is used badly. But if all moral standards are tools, there is no moral standard by which the use of any tool may be judged; any action is justified if it meets the standard of nature. And nature demands of us nothing except the satisfaction of impulse.

By this lucid bit of reasoning the radicals removed from society its Archimedean point. They dehumanized the world and reduced society to the feral pursuit of interest. They were harsh realists, and those who opposed them had no more tender reality with which to defend the human good. One hundred fifty years of political and social innovation had shattered the archaic certainties; technical mastery could not take their place. The sense of crisis is something very different from Hesiod's quiet desperation. Hesiod had a clear standard of behavior, and on his little farm he clung to the human good as he knew it. The writers of the late fifth century were possessed by doubt; they could not see the human good any more. They were faced with a choice: the inhuman world of the radicals or no world at all.

The radicals were a living disproof of the idea of progress; they were both the outcome of the whole process and its denial. The Periclean reforms, as they made people aware of the malleability of society, convinced them of its artificiality; the Periclean break with tradition led the radicals to deny any value to tradition. Pericles sought to realize the human good by sophisticating the state; his citizens became sophisticated enough to deny the human good. Power had outrun purpose, and the sophistication of the means had resulted in the denial of the end. So the radicals were not merely a problem for the present; they discredited the past. And as the past was discredited, so the future became blank; no one knew where to start again.

Man could perhaps survive, but the meaning of his survival was in question. By the development of their capacities, these men had brought themselves face to face with the void.

Let me conclude with something always dangerous: a historical analogy. We ourselves have lately concluded a long period of technical progress, marked by general optimism as to the malleability of nature and the capacity of man to create a world in conformity with his nature and capacities. Today we do not feel so optimistic. This is an analogy with a difference, for our progress has not been made in the construction of society; as far as social institutions go, we have scarcely surpassed Pericles. Our progress has been in the mastery of material nature, and we have tended to believe that if we could master material nature society would take care of itself. For us, not society but nature is primary. Nevertheless, there is an analogy, for optimism in material progress also assumes an Archimedean point. I have two last quotations; the first, from Bacon's *Advancement of Learning*, stands as the epigraph to Darwin's *Origin of Species*:

> Let no man out of a weak conceit of sobriety, or an ill-applied moderation, think or maintain, that a man can search too far or be too well studied in the book of God's word or the book of God's works; divinity or philosophy; but rather let men endeavor an endless progress or proficience in both.

For Bacon nature is God's material revelation to us, given to us for our instruction and use. As we comprehend and master the world, as we turn it to our purposes, we are using our God-given capacities to fulfil the role which God has granted us in nature. By exploiting the nature around us, we are fulfilling our own nature and completing the order of the world. Bacon's reference to God's word is perhaps only a politic nod in the direction of popular opinion; very easily nature comes to be the whole of God's gift. As man fulfils his role in nature through history, man becomes God-like; the highest of all God's creatures, he rightly perfects himself by becoming king of his own world.

But the notion of material progress assumes an order of nature, prior to our transformation of the world and independent of it. Otherwise our actions are random; our mastery of nature will bend to our good only if we are at the same time responding to the good order of nature. Nature sets out the path and man follows it; in creating a second nature, he is merely fulfilling the potential of the first. The human world completes the natural world. So the order of nature (not itself a fact of nature) is our Archimedean point: it guarantees the progressive character of our activity. This idea of the order of nature is particularly important in Darwin, where the natural order is itself perfected in history. So my last quotation is from Darwin himself, from the conclusion of the *Origin of Species*:

> As all the living forms of life are descendants of those which lived long before the Cambrian epoch, we may feel certain that the ordinary succession by generation has never once been broken, and that no cataclysm has desolated the whole world. Hence we may look with some confidence to a secure future of great length. And as natural selection works solely by and for the good of each being, all corporeal and mental endowments will tend to progress towards perfection.[62]

Today we have the power to produce such a cataclysm: to destroy life or at least so to pollute the genetic pool that the work of millennia will be undone. Perhaps we are, after all, "too well studied . . . in the book of God's works." We have come where we are by exploring the natural order, and we can now, if we wish, destroy that order. With this power in our hands, we stand puzzled.

So we share with the Greeks of the late fifth century a common dilemma. What is our role in the world we have created? As they, seeking to realize the human world, created the means for dehumanizing the world, so we, seeking to perfect nature, have created the means for destroying it. Power again has out-

---

[62] Appositely quoted by J. B. Bury in his *The Idea of Progress* (New York: Macmillan Co., 1932), p. 336.

run purpose. As man has learned to dominate his world, he seems to have lost the ability to turn that domination to his own good.

For the Greeks, of course, the crisis is not the end of the story. The Greek answer was double, in practice and in theory. The practical solution was the moderate, unexciting Hellenistic state. Questions of principle were set aside, and politics fell into the hands of a new caste of professional politicians, lacking, certainly, the vision of a Pericles but quite capable of running an ordinary society without resorting to radical measures. Most men withdrew from public life into their own houses and into their minds. So the important creations were in theory. Out of the Greek crisis came the Platonic philosophy and with it Plato's social invention, the university. These we have with us still. Perhaps we also will be able to create something as enduring, perhaps not. It is not for a historian to say.

INDEX